THE GREATEST TREASURE IN THE UNIVERSE

The Knowledge of the Glory of God in the Face of Jesus Christ

N. A. Woychuk, M. A., TH. D.

Executive Director of
Scripture Memory Fellowship

Author: "Messiah! A New Look at the Composer, the Music
and the Message," "Building Gold," "The British Josiah,"
"Abide in Me," etc.

Preface by
David Quine

Cover by
Jeffery Terpstra

SMF PRESS
P.O. Box 411551 • St. Louis, MO 63141

ISBN 1-880960-54-0

Dedicated

To my sister *Mary Woychuk*

and to my brother *William Woychuk*

whose love and friendship have been my
special portion all through life

Table of Contents

"A Sense of Him"

Not merely by the words you say,
    Not only in your deeds confessed
But in the most unconscious way
    Is Christ expressed.

Is it a beatific smile?
    A holy light upon your brow?
Oh, no—I felt His presence while
    You laughed just now.

For me 'twas not the truth you taught,
    To you so clear, to me still dim,
But when you came to me you brought
    A sense of Him.

And from your eyes He beckons me
    And from your heart His love is shed,
Till I lose sight of you, and see
    The Christ instead.

—Beatrice Cleland

Preface

You will find blessing in reading all the chapters of this book, but I wish to draw attention particularly to the last chapter.

Do we as believers in the 21st century know the surpassing riches found in the face of Christ Jesus? Have we set our minds upon the "riches of His glory"? And finally, do we comprehend in some measure the meaning of this "treasure" that we have in "earthen vessels"?

For more than fifty years Dr. Woychuk has faithfully, carefully, and clearly explained the living Word of God to us. He has never just presented ideas and once more with great skill he gently guides and leads us into the fuller knowledge of the glory of God.

If you are unaware of this "treasure," I recommend your careful and prayerful reading of this book.

Until we fully comprehend the fullness of what we have, we must ask God to shine His light into our hearts so that we too can enter into the "light of the knowledge of the glory of God in the face of Jesus Christ."

May the reading of this book shed light upon all that we have in Christ.

Dr. Woychuk, thank you for your faithful labor of love by once again opening the Scripture to us so that we might better understand the meaning of this "treasure" and share it with others.

For the glory of God.

David Quine
October 10, 2003

Chapter I

The Christian's Clear Perspective

"Therefore seeing we have this ministry, as we have received mercy, we faint not . . . For which cause we faint not; but though our outward man perish, yet the inward man is renewed day by day. For our light affliction, which is but for a moment, worketh for us a far more exceeding and eternal weight of glory; while we look not at the things which are seen, but at the things which are not seen: for the things which are seen are temporal; but the things which are not seen are eternal" (2 Cor. 4:1, 16-18).

"We faint not!" What an inspiring spirit!

We are not downhearted in our ministry! We are "always abounding in the work of the Lord."

This is the testimony of the faithful servant of Jesus Christ. He is not concerned about his own comfort or pleasure, nor is he ambitious for personal fame. He is zealous regarding the honor of his Lord, is meticulous in his care not to depart from His instructions, and makes his Master's business preeminent. He bears patiently with ridicule, prejudice and misunderstanding; he endures suffering and loss rather than compromise the interest of his Lord.

This representative of Heaven is amazing people by the undeviating manner in which he proclaims the message of his Master; and with such passionate fervor and holy enthusiasm he pleads the cause of Christ with men as "though God did beseech" (2 Cor. 5:20) them through him.

"Good and faithful servant!" (Matt. 25:21, 23).

But what is the secret of such a victorious life? What is the background of such unwavering devotion? What is the explanation of such thorough diligence?

Here is the answer:

"For which cause we faint not; but though our outward man perish, yet the inward man is renewed day by day. For our light affliction, which is but for a moment, worketh for us a far more exceeding and eternal weight of glory; while we look not at the things which are seen, but at the things which are not seen: for the things which are seen are temporal; but the things which are not seen are eternal" (2 Cor. 4:16-18).

The explanation lies in the influence of "the things which are not seen." "What is it," asked a pagan named *Adrianus*, "that makes Christians bear such sufferings?"

"The unseen things" was the reply: and that reply led to his salvation and martyrdom.

Influence of Things Not Seen

Having escaped the trying ordeal of Doubting Castle, *Christian* and *Hopeful, in Bunyan's* "Pilgrim's Progress," soon came to the Delectable Mountains, anxiously inquiring, "Is there in this place relief for pilgrims that are weary and faint in the way?"

Shepherds, whose names were *Knowledge, Experience, Watchful* and *Sincere,* were God's messengers of mercy in the Mountains Delectable; they took the pilgrims by the hand, and satisfied them with many good things. Now the pilgrims had a desire to proceed with their heavenly pilgrimage, and the Shepherds said one to another, "Let us here show to the pilgrims the Gates of the Celestial City, if they have skill to look through our Perspective-Glass."

The pilgrims gladly accepted the offer.

"So they had them to the top of an high hill, called *Clear,* and gave them their glass to look."

With exhilaration the pilgrims gained their perspective and gazed toward the Celestial City. "They thought they saw something like the Gate, and also some of the Glory of the place. Then they went away and sang this song.

"Thus by the Shepherds secrets are revel'd,
Which from all other men are kept conceal'd;
Come to the Shepherds then, if you would see
Things deep, things hid, and that mysterious be."

The pilgrims on earth are faced with the invitation of two spheres, the appeal of two worlds—"the things which are seen," and "the things which are not seen."

Let us explore for a moment the world *"of things which are seen"*: Feverishly and anxiously these human beings struggle after "What shall we eat? What shall we drink? Wherewithal shall we be clothed?" (Matt. 6:31). During the youthful years hopes are high and expectations run down long roads of dreams and visions. But one by one they are weighed down and entangled with this world's "cares, its riches and its pleasures." Disillusioned often, baffled and wearied, they continue their search in the world after something that would satisfy their thirsting souls fulfilling the "lust of the flesh, and the lust of the eyes, and the pride of life" (1 Jn. 2:16).

Almost without knowing it, they have capitulated to the immediate appeal of the things that are seen, the onslaught of this world's activities until their spiritual vision is impaired and their spiritual desires are dulled. They have ordered their manner in line with the standards of this world's materialistic society.

Distrust of the supernatural, insistence on the present and the practical, and the pride of a "self-styled common sense" are the tenets of this world's creed. The so-called "common sense" is very aggressive, and in every issue it rears itself against the promises of our God. They begin to look and feel foolish in their simple devotion to unseen realities.

But amidst all of his proud and pleasurable display, the worldling is confronted with a most startling observation, which makes him bite the dust in unwilling humiliation: "the things which are seen are *temporal.*" This world of "stuff and things" is "temporary," "transient": it lasts but for a brief season. The fickle joys quickly change into weird cries of despair. The fondest schemes of man are frustrated by time. No wonder the poet observes, "This world is all a fleeting show for man's illusion given."

"The things which are seen" have that serious lack. They are essentially insecure, characterized by instability and temporariness. Such are the nations of the world as well. They rise and fall with time. A nation rises from obscurity, plays for a little time its part upon the human stage, and then passes into obscurity again. So went Egypt, Assyria, Persia, Greece, Rome, so the proud empires of recent dictators; however impregnable they seemed, they were only sand houses built by children on the seashore. The vast security "sputniks" away.

Ordinary eyes and unenlightened minds cannot see spiritual realities. "A cat may look at a king—,but a cat can never see a king" is *Ruskin's* way of saying that there are values which some never see because they are not external in character.

> *"Father of lights, Whose Word dispelled earth's*
> *shadows,*
> *Who gavest unto man the gift of sight,*
> *Revealing by that gift what else were hidden,*
> *The world Thy power had clothed in radiance bright.*
>
> *"Grant such a revelation of eternal glory*
> *That earthly bliss before its glow shall fade;*
> *That grief may lose its sting and sin its glamour,*
> *Because our hearts on Heaven and God are stayed."*
> *—Adelina Fermi*

Most of us are familiar with the song of the Blind Ploughman in which he tells how "God took my eyes away that I might see," and he speaks, presumably, of seeing spiritual values,—outstretching continents of eternal heavenly delights.

Fanny Crosby, the great hymn-writer, when she was a few weeks old, became blind through a doctor's blunder. Eighty-three years afterward she wrote: "I verily believe it was God's intention that

I should live my days in physical darkness, so as to be better prepared to sing His praises." And the poet *Milton* wrote regarding his blindness:

"So much the rather thou celestial light
Shine inward, and the mind through all her powers
Irradiate, there plant eyes, all mist from thence
Purge and disperse, that I may see and tell
Of things invisible to mortal sight."

"We faint not," says the Apostle triumphantly, "but though the outward man perish, yet the inward man is renewed day by day . . . While we LOOK at the things which are not seen." We must steadfastly focus our interest upon those abiding, eternal verities which lie beyond the glitter of these transient things that constantly clamor for our attention. This look must be resolute. "Set your affection on things above," the Apostle urges, and "not on things on the earth" (Col. 3:2).

The Reality of Things Not Seen

And what are some of these enthralling *things unseen,* which stand out clear and constant to faith's vision?

First is the *wonderful Lord Himself.* "Whom having not seen, ye love; in whom, though now ye see Him not, yet believing, ye rejoice with joy unspeakable and full of glory" (1 Pet. 1:8).

2) The unceasing thrill of *knowing that our sins are forgiven,* and that we are "accepted in the Beloved," and that our sure destiny is heaven.

3) The substantial satisfaction which comes from the *realization of usefulness.*

4) The indescribable delight of *personal, direct communion with God* in prayer, in meditation upon His Word, and in calm stillness before Him.

5) The *cheering confidence* of knowing that God "shall supply all our needs" from day to day. Freedom from want. Freedom from fear. Freedom from anxious care. "We have all and abound" (Phil. 4).

6) The "*new song* in our hearts," the "*blessed hope*" of seeing the Lord face to face.

We see how that "our afflictions" are really "light" and but for "a moment," and more amazing still, we notice that in the wonderful providence of God these afflictions "work for us a far more exceeding and eternal weight of glory."

Our frail bodies suffer pain and quickly tend to decay; we pass amidst sorrow and weeping and death itself, but "we sorrow not as others who have no hope"; the light of Eternity enables us to see life and death in their true perspectives.

Perspective of Faith Illustrated

Against such a background of indescribable

glories spreading out into eternity, *our ministry looms large!*

"By faith" Enoch walked with God, and one day walked right into heaven with Him. Enoch did not taste death. In his walk of faith he was translated into the very presence of God and "he had witness borne to him that before his translation he had been well-pleasing unto God" (Heb. 11:5 ASV). God was delighted with Enoch's faith in His promises. God attested his faith. God *bore him witness* that his faith was approved.

"By faith Abraham, when he was called to go out into a place which he should after receive for an inheritance, obeyed; and he went out, not knowing whither he went" (Heb. 11:8).

The divine call had been to Abraham and he "staggered not at the promise of God through unbelief." There was no question about the promise of God, but there were no external helps to make him certain of its fulfillment; it had no encouragement. The entire trend of circumstances frowned upon it. Common sense was opposed to the promise of God and to Abraham's venture. Yet Abraham "was strong in faith." He examined the promise and steadied himself upon it, and he was "giving God the glory" (Rom. 4:20).

He "staggered not"; he was sustained by his confidence in "the things which are not seen." He was "fully persuaded that, what He had promised, He was able also to perform." "By faith he sojourned in the land of promise, as in a strange country," where in numerous ways he tested the promises of God and found them sufficient.

Look at Moses. By faith he attained the spiritual stature of a spiritual giant.

"By faith" he perceived the essential nature of the "pleasures of sin," that they do not really satisfy the soul and that they are only "for a season."

"By faith" he considered the "reproach of Christ" far superior and more to be desired than the "treasures of Egypt."

"By faith" the rewards of eternity assumed for him a present and precious reality: "he had respect unto the recompense of the reward."

And the record of his life, his faith and his unparalleled leadership of God's chosen earthly people is well known to all of us.

"He endured as seeing Him who is invisible!"

"For this cause we faint not!"

"We look at things not seen." We see Him who is invisible, even Jesus, ". . . the author and finisher of our faith; who for the joy that was set before Him endured the cross, despising the shame, and is set down at the right hand of the throne of God" (Heb. 12:2).

"Your Calling, Brethren"

"Therefore seeing we have this ministry, as we have received mercy, we faint not." We have it. It is for everyone who has received mercy; it is a ministry for every believer. The beloved missionary, *Judson*, was known as "Jesus Christ's man." Every Christian is a "Christ man."

Every human being who has been born of the Spirit of God is an instrument of righteousness. Every person who has been redeemed by the precious blood of Christ is a missionary of the Cross. Everyone who has been reconciled to God by simple faith in Jesus Christ as Savior is a fully commissioned ambassador of Christ. Every individual, who by the wonder-working power of God has been translated from the kingdom of darkness into the kingdom of light and life, is a minister. Every man, woman, boy or girl who has been saved by the grace of God is henceforth His bondservant, His agent, His emissary, His witness.

Every Christian is a *witness*; every believer is a *minister*; every saint is an *ambassador*; every child of God is a *missionary*! Christians, we cannot possibly escape this responsibility. If we have been made new creatures by His resurrection power, and have been possessed by His Spirit, we shall never be able to deny the high calling as His ministers.

Now, it is true that we may be *undependable* witnesses, *unfruitful* ministers, *unfaithful* ambassadors, *unwilling* missionaries, and waste most of our life in selfish pursuits; but, nevertheless, it is quite impossible for us to deny our calling.

Indeed, these are the orders of our Lord: "Go ye therefore, and teach all nations" (Matt. 28:19); "Ye shall be witnesses unto Me both in Jerusalem, and in all Judaea, and in Samaria, and unto the uttermost part of the earth" (Acts 1:8); "For the love of Christ constraineth us . . . Now then we are ambassadors for Christ, as though God did beseech you by us" (2 Cor. 5:14, 20). "Herein is my Father glorified, that ye bear much fruit; so shall ye be My disciples . . . Ye have not chosen Me, but I have chosen you, and ordained you, that ye should go and bring forth fruit, and that your fruit should remain" (Jn. 15:8, 16).

In the Old Testament economy, the spiritual ministry was largely limited to prophets and priests. Then came our great high priest, the Lord Jesus Christ, who "loved us, and washed us from our sins in His own blood, and hath made us kings and priests unto God" (Rev. 1:5, 6). Christ brought to an end all the sacrificial rites of the old economy when He offered Himself as the all-atoning, sufficient sacrifice for our sin. In so doing the Old Testament priesthood system was dissolved, and in His sight all believers were placed on the same level—"a chosen generation, a royal priesthood,... a peculiar people; that ye should show forth the praises of Him who hath called you out of darkness into His marvellous light" (1 Pet. 2:9).

We are all God's ministers. The seal of Christ to this end is upon every believer. We are all instruments, servants, agencies, through whom God would speak and illustrate to the whole world the power of His living and redeeming Word. Christ's stamp is upon every agent whom He sends forth. His call, His anointing, His sign of authority is burned into the character of everyone born from above. As our Lord commissioned Paul, even so in a very real sense it is true concerning every servant of God.

This is the plan of God for the growth and spiritual progress of every individual therein "unto the measure of the stature of the fulness of Christ."

The record of how the early Christians functioned and fulfilled this ministry is both stimulating and instructive:

Andrew "came and saw," and then at once goes out to find "his own brother Simon, and *saith* unto him, We have found the Messias, which is, being interpreted, the Christ" (Jn. 1:41).

"Philip findeth Nathanael, and *saith* unto him, We have found Him."

The woman of Samaria, who received "that living water" and in whom was opened up the irresistible fountain of upspringing water of life, "left her waterpot, and went her way into the city, and *saith* to the men, Come, see a man, which told me all things that ever I did" (Jn. 4:28, 29).

And the man who had been blind from his birth "came seeing" after the miracle-anointing of the blessed Lord, and then triumphantly rang out his testimony before that crowd of skeptics and religious bigots, "One thing I know, that, whereas I was blind, now I see" (Jn. 9:25).

The redeemed of the Lord have been silent far too long. We want believers who are unafraid to speak out for the Lord in season and out of season. Oh assembly of saints, why this speechlessness? Awake, and let every man proclaim the good news of salvation. "Let the redeemed of the Lord say so." Every Christian can at all times relate his own experience, modestly and tenderly, as to the work of grace in his heart. A person may not be able to interpret prophecies and expound the deep mysteries so that a thousand men shall listen in rapt attention, but everyone can tell what he has seen and known and felt and handled of the Word of life!

"We also Believe, and Therefore Speak"

There are too many of those silent, secret disciples in our day who make a merit of their silence, and boast of the fact that they have never by a single syllable betrayed their faith. They are unmindful of how seriously they are betraying their faith by their ungrateful silence.

The Psalmist of old said, "I believed, therefore have I spoken" (Psa. 116:10). The Apostle Paul utilizes this approach in this very chapter of Second Corinthians by quoting the Psalmist and then thundering out *"We also believe, and therefore speak"* (4:13).

If those who have experienced the power of the gospel in their own lives will not speak of it, who will? "Ye are the salt of the earth; ye are the light of the world; ye are cities set upon a hill."

This is the means by which the spirit of God would reach the weary multitudes with the balm of the gospel. God's provisions are sufficient for every exigency of human life, for every aspect of our experience, for every anticipation of human hope. Here is a psalm for encouragement for the sorrowing; here is a promise of rest for the weary; here is a needed stimulus for the indolent; here is a benediction for the aged and instruction for the children. Yes, "rivers of living water" are to flow out from the children of God in all directions for healing and for blessing.

Not a day passes but every Christian is given a wonderful opportunity of proclaiming the gospel. And it is the utilizing of such opportunities by the rank and file of believers which will put the Church of Jesus Christ on the march in an invincible, conquering offensive which shall result in the salvation of the downhearted, confused multitudes around us.

"We have this ministry!"

"We also believe, and therefore speak!"

The man who truly believes in Christ feels that a sort of inward, impelling "necessity is laid upon him," so that he "cannot but speak the things seen and heard." His faith is like a deep, unfathomed spring; his words and his witness, then, become like an irrepressible stream.

God, give us dependable witnesses, fruitful ministers, faithful ambassadors, willing and winning missionaries—servants of God in whom the divine fire is burning so that we shall indeed consider ourselves to be under the mighty power of the Holy Spirit.

"We have this ministry."

"For ye see your calling, brethren, how that not many wise men after the flesh, not many mighty, not many noble, are called: But God hath chosen the foolish things of the world to confound the wise; and God hath chosen the weak things of the world to confound the things which are mighty; and base things of the world, and things which are despised, hath God chosen, yea, and things which are not, to bring to nought things that are: that no flesh should glory in His presence" (1 Cor. 1:26-29).

Chapter II

The Large-Type Christian

*"Therefore seeing we have this minis-
try, as we have received mercy, we faint
not; but have renounced the hidden things
of dishonesty, not walking in craftiness,
nor handling the word of God deceitfully;
but by manifestation of the truth commending ourselves to every man's conscience in the sight of God" (2 Cor. 4:1, 2).*

The Apostle's deep concern is not so much "to tell out the truth as it is to make the truth tell."

"To make the truth tell." To make the truth of the gospel telling and effective.

His object is not to frame an unanswerable argument, but to produce an irresistible impression—an impression which subdues the soul, and lays hold of the conscience.

This verse strikes at the heart of the believer, and makes him realize some of the things that are necessary if his life is to reflect the gospel of Christ effectively. He is under divine authority to "manifest" the truth. Not simply to proclaim it, but to exhibit the truth, to commend it with his whole life in such a way that the Spirit of God may readily use it as the "power of God unto salvation to every one that believeth."

Throughout all his letters the Apostle Paul presses this idea home. He says to the saints in America and in Canada, as well as to those in Corinth, "Ye are our epistle . . . known and read of all men . . . written not with ink, but with the Spirit of the living God" (2 Cor. 3:2, 3).

The Holy Spirit wishes to write the truth of the gospel upon our lives in large, bold letters. The spiritual perception of the natural man is weak. His eyes are dim to spiritual truth. Satan continually thrusts the "veil" before him. The edition of the "large-type" Christians is small. A greater supply is needed. I mean Christians who can be read at a glance, even by those whose eyesight for this sort of thing is usually poor. We must not put any strain upon them. We must make it easy for them to see the message, however hastily they rush along.

How can we do it? Not, of course, by sanctimonious phrases, by peculiarities of dress, nor by ostentatious charities; not merely by holding ourselves aloof from certain activities; not by hermit-like isolation; not by observing accusingly the weaknesses of our brethren. Yea, rather, we become *large-type Christians* by thorough-going honesty, which scorns alike the crooked customs of the world and the inward hypocrisy of the church member; by a truthfulness as straightforward and as enlightening as the sunlight; by a genuine sympathy which comes as a blessed balm of healing to many a wounded spirit; by a cheerful faithfulness in the task which God has ordained for us to perform. Such a testimony, joined with an open, simple confession of eternal life through Christ, will stand out in bold relief. When the words of salvation are backed up by such a life, no one has difficulty in perceiving the stamp of Christ. The seal of the Holy Spirit is impressed so strongly and so clearly on such souls that even they who run may read it.

David Livingstone is an excellent example of a *large-type Christian*.

The great English explorer of Africa, *Sir Henry M. Stanley*, who found Livingstone in the heart of the dark continent, tells the story of his conversion as follows:

"I went to Africa as prejudiced against religion as the worst infidel in London. To a reporter like myself, who had only to deal with wars, mass meetings, and political gatherings, sentimental matters were quite out of my province. But there came to me a long time for reflection. I was out there away from a worldly world. I saw this solitary old man (Livingstone) there, and I asked myself, 'Why does he stop here in such a place? What is it that inspires him?'

"For months after we met I found myself listening to him, wondering at the old man carrying out the words, 'Leave all, and follow Me.' But little by little, seeing his piety, his gentleness, his zeal, his earnestness, and how he went quietly about his business, I was converted by him, although he had not tried in any way to do it."

"Let your light so shine!" Every action, every word, and every thought impelled and controlled by God's grace is a message.

"We preach not ourselves, but Christ Jesus the Lord." We preach not ourselves, but we do preach *with* ourselves.

"Have Renounced the Hidden Things of Dishonesty"

Every believer who would be a large-type Christian must engage in this honest, outright judgment of self, renouncing "the hidden things of dishonesty." The Apostle urges, "Get at those shameful and disgraceful hidden things," which make ineffectual your witness and which cause you to faint.

Those "hidden things of dishonesty" creep into the lives of all God's children, even those with the finest intentions. Old *Job* declared an excellent resolution when he said, "My heart shall not reproach me so long as I live" (27:6), but he soon found occasion to lament his inward corruption and defilement.

Themistocles could not sleep because of the

multitudes that filled the streets of Athens and the laurels that they brought whenever *Miltiades* came out.

Ananias and *Sapphira* could not be at peace because of the praises that were poured upon Barnabas by the Apostles, and by all the poor. So, like Barnabas, they sold their possession, and supposedly, like Barnabas, they laid the price of it at Peter's feet. They were thrilled at the impression they were making. "Yes, lay it at Peter's feet," we imagine Sapphira saying to her hesitating husband, "and say that you are very sorry that the land did not sell for far more. After I have made my purchases, I will join you there in good time for the breaking of bread and for prayers. Keep a place for me at the Table."

Ananias wasn't entirely happy as he approached Peter with his misrepresented bounty. It struck him like a thunderbolt, when Peter, instead of smilingly approving him, denounced him to his face, "Ananias, why hath Satan filled thine heart to lie to the Holy Ghost?"

And the young men carried him out and buried him.

Three hours later Sapphira joined her husband, and they were buried in Aceldama, next door to Judas, the proprietor of the place, as it were. Let us hope that they were stricken in a "sanctifying discipline" of the household of faith, rather than in an everlasting condemnation. As *Jeremy Taylor* remarks, "God sometimes directs a temporal death in order to keep others from an eternal one."

How immense and sobering this!

Barnabas cannot sell his estate and lay the price of it at Peter's feet, but by doing so he stirs up envy in the church, and two "good" people are taken in tragic death. Why, Ananias and Sapphira envisioned sitting at the Lord's table till Peter preached their funeral sermon, and praised them for their generosity and noble example. But Peter knew the processes of Satan. He knew it by experience. He speaks with indignation. But, unfortunately, neither Ananias nor Sapphira had recovered sufficiently from the envy-complex to go out and "weep bitterly" and return to the communion table.

When men would praise us for our generosity, for our sermons, for our faith, let us think of Ananias and Sapphira. Let us think twice before we say so innocently, "This is all I can spare; indeed, this is all I possess." When men would praise us, let us heed old *Fenelon's* oft-repeated counsel, *"Seek obscurity, seek obscurity."*

> *"Search me, O God, and know my heart today;*
> *Try me, O Savior, know my thoughts I pray:*
> *See if there be some wicked way in me:*
> *Cleanse me from ev'ry sin, and set me free."*

Remember Simon Magus? He was that famous "convert" of deacon Philip in Samaria. Simon Magus was probably about to commence a nationwide preaching and healing campaign. He was a very clever man, and at the same time a very bad man, but by his pious pretensions, he had the whole of Samaria at his feet, saying, "This man is the great power of God" (Acts 8:9, 10). Prior to his supposed conversion, Simon Magus bewitched the people with sorcery, giving it out that he himself was some great one. When he posed conversion, and was baptized, Philip was taken in by it, and perhaps flashed a wire to Jerusalem, "Brethren, a man wicked like the devil himself was converted, and has been baptized by me."

On hearing this, the Apostles sent up two of their foremost men to survey the movement. The Holy Spirit went with them, and equipped them with special miracle-working powers like those which the Lord exercised in order to attract attention to His ministry at a time when the world was steeped in total darkness. The Holy Ghost came upon them through the ministry of the Apostles, and there was great rejoicing and praise to God.

Meanwhile, Simon Magus was greatly impressed with what he saw. Neither did he stand by idly. He must have been chairman of some important campaign committee. He rated a special introduction to the Apostles, perhaps, as the greatest gambler convert in the land. But despite all that he saw and heard he was never converted. He was smitten with the tremendous opportunity that all this business afforded for making big money. He was still more intoxicated with the love of notoriety. Is not he, Simon Magus, "the great power of God"? His name must continue to be on people's lips. He must draw the large crowds. The many people that hung on the words of Peter and John and followed them from place to place were gall and wormwood to Simon Magus. Says *Alexander Whyte*, "Popularity was the very breath of life to that charlatan of Samaria."

Peter kept a watchful eye on the "big" convert, and probably detected a slight counterfeit shade in his "very spiritual" make-up. Then came the night when it came right out. Simon Magus slams down a bag of money on the table, and says, "Give me also this power."

The sight of the bag, and the blasphemous proposal must have nearly driven Peter beside himself, as he blazed out at the wretched mossback with a fiery denunciation, "Thy money perish with thee . . . thy heart is not right in the sight of God . . . thou art in the gall of bitterness, and in the bond of iniquity . . . Repent!" (Acts 8:9-25)

It is easy for you and me to dismiss the

hypocritical dissimulation of Simon Magus, but not so this wicked heart of mine that never seems rid of the desire for the praise of men. How we need to flee from the adulation and applause that loving, appreciative servants of God would heap upon us. Again *Whyte*, "Never search the papers to see what they are saying about you. Starve the self-seeking quack that is still within you."

> *"I praise Thee, Lord, for cleansing me from sin:*
> *Fulfill Thy Word, and make me pure within;*
> *Fill me with fire, where once I burned with shame:*
> *Grant my desire to magnify Thy name."*

Before we pass on to the next section, let us observe one of our Lord's parable characters, the laborer with the evil eye (Matt. 20:1-16). *Aesop's* dog in the manger had his own bone, and undoubtedly it was both big and juicy. But he was such a hound at heart that he could not stand to see his master's ox munch on a little straw without snarling and snapping at him. Now, the snarling laborer with the "evil eye" did not complain that he was underpaid. It was this: "These last have wrought but one hour, and thou hast made them equal unto us, which have borne the burden and heat of the day." All his misery came from this, that his fellow-servant was so much overpaid. "Both Aesop's dog, and our Lord's doglike laborer, were sick of that strange disease,—their neighbor's health." This laborer's evil heart was running out of his evil eye, and his lips gave words to that perversity. Oh, the hellishness of envy that comes upon the saints of God! There are those who can't stand to see their neighbor or "rival" prosper in any way.

"As to the motive of those attacks on *Goethe*," says *Heine*, "I know at least what it was in my own case. It was my evil eye." Now, who is your Goethe? The tone of your voice, the very cough of your throat, and shifting of the eyes betrays that "evil eye," when that certain person is favorably in view.

And to think that this whole parable on the laborer with the "evil eye" was given to bare the wicked motive of the Apostle Peter when he said, "Behold, we have forsaken all, and followed Thee; what shall we have therefore?"

It is the inward reasonings of our hearts that matter so much with the Lord. He would have us examine again and again—yea, never cease judging assiduously—those "hidden things of dishonesty." The motive counts more with Him than strength, or skill, or success in His laborers.

God grant that we may be constantly on the alert regarding the desperate wickedness of our own hearts, "lest Satan should get an advantage of us: for we are not ignorant of his devices" (2 Cor. 2:11). Beware how you shield yourself from yourself, and how you use "distinctions" when you are debating with your conscience about yourself. Watch intently the attitude of your heart even in the matter of confessing your sin.

Whyte cites the example of Julius, which, in reality is you and me, after this fashion: "Julius goes to prayers, he confesses himself to be a miserable sinner, he accuses himself to God with all the aggravations that can be, as having no health in him; yet Julius cannot bear to be informed of any imperfection, or suspected to be wanting in any degree of virtue. Now, can there be stronger proof that Julius is wanting in sincerity of his devotions? Is not this a plain sign that his confessions to God are only words of course, and humble civility of speech to His Maker, in which his heart has no share? Julius confesses himself to be in great weakness, corruption, disorder, and infirmity, and yet is angry at any one that does but suppose *his defection* in any virtue. Is it not the same thing as if he had said, You must not imagine that I am in earnest in my devotion?"

If there be those brethren who regard themselves as having become sufficiently matured to outgrow such treachery and internal deceit, let me point you to the Apostles of our Lord. It was the night before His crucifixion, while they ate the last Passover. "And as they did eat, He said, Verily I say unto you, that one of you shall betray Me. And they were exceeding sorrowful, and began every one of them to say unto Him, Lord, is it I?" (Matt. 26:21, 22).

"One of you shall betray me." Our Lord's statement awakened doubt, misgiving, fear, surprise, anger, resentment, according to the character of each disciple. *Leonardo da Vinci,* great Italian painter, with keen insight into the pathos of that last night together, has so fixed the expression of each Apostle in "The Last Supper," that they still speak to us out of his masterpiece, as indeed it is recorded in the Word. One after another they said, "Lord, is it I?"

It is indeed a strange commentary on our fallen nature that our Lord's words should have so aroused questioning in the hearts of all His disciples. Probably each one was deeply in earnest with the question, with the exception of Judas, who had already sold himself off to the devil. It appears that not one of them was quite sure of his own loyalty in every respect.

The Negro spiritual refrain touches a responsive chord in the heart of every sincere believer, "Not my father, not my mother; not my sister, not my brother; but it's me, O Lord, standing in the need of prayer."

Jeremiah is divinely and entirely right about the resentment, the dishonesty, the malice, the pride, the envy, the hatred, the ill-will of our hearts toward all who have ever hindered us, or injured us, or detracted us, or refused to flatter us. Desperately and deceivingly, and down to the death, wicked and undependable heart!

What shall we do? Where shall we go?

Thank God, who giveth us the victory, day by day, and hour by hour, through our Lord Jesus Christ! Thanks be unto God! Ah, there's the secret. The spirit of implicit trust only in the Lord, the spirit of constant looking unto Jesus for that needed strength, the spirit of realizing that strength, and thanking Him for it.

"Not Walking in Craftiness nor Handling the Word of God Deceitfully"—

In this Scripture, crafty conduct is paired with "adulterating the Word of God." These two ever go together. He who is not honest with himself will not be very honest with the Word. The reverse is also true. Cunning deception to gain one's end by underhanded means and dishonest methods is bad enough, but, when falsifying the Word of God is added thereto, it makes for the most dastardly evil in the sight of God.

We dare not tamper with His truth. We are not to trim doctrines in order to commend ourselves to the fancies and predilections of men. Juggling of truth may please men not a little, but the gospel truth proclaimed and exhibited earnestly will convict them.

Preachers, as well as others, sometimes become tricksters in the way they handle the things of God. They season the truth according to the tastes of the carnal. They keep back those portions which might offend the rich and the influential sinners. Christ's ambassadors become diplomatists and strategists, rather than heralds. They manipulate their message. They adapt it to the spirit of the time, or the prejudices of their hearers. The end of all this artifice and ingenuity is self-gain and self-recommendation.

However, no matter how ingenious we are in covering up our evil motive, it has a strange way of revealing itself in our walk and in our talk. It "peeps out." Counterfeit Christianity is no less difficult to put across successfully than is counterfeit money.

But "let him that thinketh he standeth take heed lest he fall." The human heart is "deceitful and desperately wicked." That refers to your heart and mine. It takes in also the perverse heart of Balaam.

To begin with, Balaam was a true and greatly gifted prophet of Almighty God, but for all his fine sermons he had his price, and the "god of this world" tripped him up with the shimmering prospect of "gold and honor" (Num. 22-25).

Balak, the king of Moab, was distressed because of the strength of the children of Israel. Therefore he sends messengers to Balaam with the petition that Balaam come over and curse the children of Israel and cause their defeat. God makes His will plain and simple to Balaam: *"Thou shalt not go with them; thou shalt not curse the people: for they are blessed."*

So Balaam gives his answer, "Get you into your land: for the Lord refuseth to give me leave to go with you." A good answer, but somehow Balaam's inward greed *peeped out.* It left the impression that Balaam might be willing, but God "refuseth: to give him the needed sanction. Poor Balaam, the sharp hook is already near his mouth, and an hour or two of smart manipulation, and the fool will be in Satan's basket.

Balak is a strong believer in what "gold" can do. The god of this world's gold has made him that way. He believes in it. So he sends to Balaam for information, "Wherewith shall I come before the Lord, and bow myself before the high God? shall I come before Him with burnt offerings, with calves of a year old? Will the Lord be pleased with thousands of rams, or with ten thousands of rivers of oil?"

What a mercenary, calculating, brazen approach!

Notice the answer. Balaam answers him, "He hath showed thee, O man, what is good; and what doth the Lord require of thee, but to do justly, and to love mercy, and to walk humbly with thy God" (Micah 6:5-8).

A wonderful answer. Neither Moses, nor David, nor Isaiah, nor Paul himself could have answered better.

But Balaam's dishonest heart had "peeped out," and so Balak dangles the bait: "I will promote thee unto very great honour, and I will do whatsoever thou sayest unto me: come therefore, I pray thee, curse me this people."

Now hear a mighty declaration from a man whose deceitful heart already had him on the skids downward: "If Balak would give me his house full of silver and gold, I cannot go beyond the word of the Lord my God, to do less or more." Like many preachers, Balaam put all his tears into his voice, and all his contrition went into his loud public confession.

Oh the deceitfulness of the human heart! Satan seems to lurk in every corner waiting for an opportunity. And none of us is equal for his wiles did we confide in our own resources.

Now, look at the devilish turn of Balaam's deceived and deceiving heart. He turns to Balak's persistent envoys and says, "Tarry ye also here this night, that I may know what the Lord will say unto me more." Look out, the hook is now in the mouth!

Balaam is on his knees all night praying to know God's will! What a travesty. Why, he already knew God's will. God had explicitly told him, and Balaam had just as explicitly declared it to Balak's solicitors. Had Balaam put away "the hidden things of dishonesty" and had he been willing to talk faithfully before his God, he would have refused so much as to see Balak's second deputation of messengers, and made it clear that Balak had his last answer already. But Balaam wanted a great name and a great fortune.

So he prays all night, not to know God's will, but how to get around God's will. A great deal of our anxiety, and perplexity, and strong pleading, and eager supplication is made up of that same brand of self-deceit. It reminds me of the preacher who received a call to another church with a substantial salary increase. On Monday morning a deacon called on the pastor whose little boy came to the door and reported that "Daddy is busy praying to know God's will about the call." "Then, may I see your mother?" inquired the deacon. "No," said the boy, "she is busy upstairs packing."

It is now morning, and Balaam is still agonizing in prayer!

"Beholding Balaam's insincerity," says *Philo*,

"and being angry at it, God said, by all means go, Balaam." Yes, surely! Our God does not place us under lock and key. He does not tie up our hands and feet. He does not strike us lame to enforce obedience. He endowed us with a free will. He respects it. Yes, He says, you know what I've said, now choose for yourself. Where is your treasure? What is it you really want? Sure, "if the men come to call thee, rise up, and go with them."

There goes a thoroughly dishonest prophet, mumbling to himself as he goes, largely to mollify his conscience, "If Balak would give me his house full of silver and gold, I cannot go beyond the word of the Lord." But in his heart he wishes there were some way in which he could get all that gold. There is, Balaam! And if you set your heart on it, the way will come, and you will get your heap of gold, and still retain an *outward* shell of loyalty to your God!

You know the story. The angel of the Lord stood in the path, but Balaam was too blind to see it. The ass saw the angel, though, and thrust herself into the wall, and crushed Balaam's foot against the wall. The dumb ass was doing its best trying to save her eloquent master, and even talked to Balaam about his violence and stubbornness.

"Why hast thou smitten me?" pleaded the dumb brute. And Balaam exasperated in his madness shrieked, "Because thou hast mocked me." Yea, verily! Was it not Balaam who was mocking God, walking in craftiness, handling the Word of God deceitfully?

Had he not been bereft of all discernment and honesty, he would have turned the donkey's head in that narrow lane, and would have carried his crushed foot home to heal it, and to begin a new life. But Balaam was too far gone. The bait was too well lodged in his mouth! The voice of the ass, the angel of the Lord, the crushed foot, all these notwithstanding, Balaam stubbornly pushes ahead.

Have you a crushed foot tonight? I think I do. Come, let us return to the Lord our God. He has torn, and He will heal us.

Only Balaam mounted his ass again, with the help of the angel, and came to Balak. Once he arrived, Balak whisked him around from one hill-top to another in order to get the proper place from which to curse Israel. The whole situation would be a first-rate comedy were it not so marked with undertones of heartbreaking tragedy. Balaam keeps asking for altars and for sacrifices, and in-sists that he cannot go beyond the word of the Lord. Balak keeps the gold and the fame before the deceived prophet. At times they both seem desperate in trying to find a spot where they can get at their sin, without the restraints of God.

You and I may try to live the life of greed and selfishness and worldliness, and idleness, and vanity, and vice. We may neglect His Word and prayer and sincere confession, but we cannot to on for long that way. We may try to shut our eyes and let a Balak lead us among the hills of mammon, but we can never find that place where we can give our hearts over to evil, or where we can sin without an inward rebuke.

But Balaam would have Balak's gold. His foot was now whole again. Balaam was a clever man. After some underground management, Balak and Balaam must have met secretly in the dark. Balaam gave Balak the advice which produced the results Balak desired, and yet Balaam actually did not have to curse the children of Israel. It was the same advice that Belial has given again and again. Set women in their eyes, counselled the old reprobate (Deut. 31:16). The sons of Israel were corrupted "with the daughters of Moab," and "Israel joined himself unto Baal-peor: and the anger of the Lord was kindled against Israel."

Yes, and Balaam got his gold! In a similar way, we may obtain that honor, that empty fame, that position, that objective!

Jude cautions all who would run "greedily after the error of Balaam for reward." They are "clouds without water, carried about of winds: trees whose fruit withereth, without fruit, twice dead, plucked up by the roots; raging waves of the sea, foaming out their own shame" (11-13).

Let everyone of us permit the Spirit of God to discover our internal hypocrisy and our self-deceit on every turn of this winding way. Let us so look upon our Lord and Savior that our conscience will smite us because of our deeply ingrained self-love, and self-deceit.

Let Nathan's sword pierce our hearts again and again, until we cry out without show or superficiality, "Yes, Lord, I am that man. I am that man." And so let us continually disavow any confidence in ourselves. For indeed, there dwelleth no good thing in the flesh—neither in yours nor in mine. And so with every parable, with every psalm, with every prayer, with every promise let us come to the Lord, and let Him perfect His strength in our weakness.

And when you come to that glorious, quickening fifty-first psalm again, let it be the prayer, the confession, the cry of your heart, and not just the lips: "Behold, Thou desirest truth in the inward parts: and in the hidden part Thou shalt make me to know wisdom. Purge me with hyssop . . . make me to hear joy and gladness . . . Create in me a clean heart, O God; and renew a right spirit within me . . . Restore unto me the joy of Thy salvation; and uphold me with Thy free spirit. Then will I teach transgressors Thy ways; and sinners shall be converted unto Thee."

As the Lord gives us grace, and as our hearts are more and more softened, and tamed, and humbled, and sweetened by the grace of God, and by the indwelling Spirit, we may be enabled by our wonderful God to go forth against the giant, and against the bear, and against the lion in the name and in the strength of our God.

Our hearts will then be a little more ready to praise God for His goodness. Sometimes, we may even imagine seeing the man after God's own heart who abounded with thankfulness more than any other that is recorded in Scripture, with his hands upon his harp, and his eyes fixed upon heaven, calling in exultation upon all creation, upon men and angels, to join with his rapturous soul in praising the Lord of heaven. Why not sing with this divine musician a psalm that seems to express the very mood of our grateful hearts:

> *"Bless, O my soul, the Lord thy God,*
> *And not forgetful be*
> *Of all His gracious benefits*
> *He hath bestow'd on thee.*

> *"For Thou art God that dost*
> *To me salvation send,*
> *And I upon Thee all the day*
> *Expecting to attend."*

"We have renounced the hidden things of dishonesty, not walking in craftiness, nor handling

the word of God deceitfully . . . ."

"But by Manifestation of the Truth"—

Not just *any* truth, but that truth which is gathered up in the glorious story of redemption through our Lord and Savior Jesus Christ. It is the truth of God's righteousness provided for such as you and me through God's infinite love. It is the truth that makes possible God's "unspeakable gift." It is the truth that has power to convince, to convert the heart, to control the will, to constrain the life. "Know the truth," our Lord said, "and the truth shall make you free."

The Apostle Paul summed up the essence of this delivering truth thus: "Being justified freely by His grace through the redemption that is in Christ Jesus: Whom God hath set forth to be a propitiation through faith in His blood, to declare His righteousness for the remission of sins that are past, through the forbearance of God; to declare, I say, at this time His righteousness: that He might be just, and the justifier of him which believeth in Jesus" (Rom. 3:24-26).

Therefore, we herald the truth not simply as literature, nor as creeds or theories, but as eternal life through God's man, Christ Jesus.

Furthermore, we are to "manifest" the truth, which means "to make visible, to make clear, to make known." Believers are to make the gospel of Christ visible in a clear, consistent way. It does its work best when it is fully exhibited, and is permitted to radiate by its own light. Men must see the gospel as well as hear it. For that reason you and I must live it as well as talk it. "There is always more in the pulpit than the sermon—there is the man." says *Hurndall*. We naturally wonder what the gospel has done for that preacher or that deacon who so earnestly recommends it to others. We must be "doers of the Word," and not preachers only, "deceiving our own selves."

"We have renounced," the Apostle says, "all these weak ingenuities of the flesh, and exhibit the truth with a spirit of urgency and godly sincerity." The long-time beloved pastor of Moody Memorial Church, *Dr. H. A. Ironside*, said, "I have prayed thousands of times, and I dare to pray again, knowing that God may take me at my word if I fail, 'O God, keep me from ever being able to preach the gospel without a clear conscience and the power of the Holy Ghost.' "

In a Bible class recently the teacher was telling of the various translations of the Bible and the different excellencies. He spoke of Jerome's Vulgate, of the King James Version, of the Revised Version and others.

One of the class members interrupted by saying,

"I prefer my mother's translation of the Bible myself to any other version."

"Your mother's?" said the teacher, "What do you mean, Fred?"

"I mean that my mother has translated the Bible into the language of daily life for me ever since I was old enough to understand it," said Fred. "There has never been any obscurity about her version. Whatever printed version of the Bible I may study, my mother's is always the one that clears up my difficulties."

His mother was a *large-type* Christian whose whole life was a continual "manifestation of the truth."

"We have renounced the hidden things of dishonesty, not walking in craftiness, nor handling the word of God deceitfully; but by manifestation of the truth . . ."

"Commending Ourselves" —

All ordinary commendations praise the person concerned. Here is a self-recommendation that asks nothing for self, that asks everything for the truth that it reveals and publishes.

This type of self-commendation can be accomplished only through the most genuine selflessness. It involves pure motive and complete dedication. It involves a certain directness and simplicity of method. It carries with it a sense of reality and deep urgency.

The Apostle's unchanging goal was that the glorious gospel of Christ be effectively proclaimed and just as effectively be exhibited and commended by the life. "For our rejoicing is this," he said, "the testimony of our conscience, that in simplicity and godly sincerity, not with fleshly wisdom, but by the grace of God, we have had our conversation in the world, and more abundantly to you-ward" (2 Cor. 1:12).

Sometimes what we proclaim with our mouth is not commended by our life. Our big creed is distorted by our little deeds. *Thomas Carlyle*, the dour literature critic, spoke well enough when he said, "Oh, give us the man who sings at his work! One is scarcely sensible of fatigue whilst he marches to music. Wondrous is the strength of cheerfulness, altogether past calculation its powers of endurance."

Alas, Carlyle so poorly practiced this preachment of his! He himself was an apt example of *cheerlessness* and gruffness. His ways did not commend his talk.

The Apostle Paul was a wonderful example of self-commendation for the sake of the gospel. God uses Paul to give us the most vital instruction on this subject because Paul's own matchless record shines through the instruction. Hear him:

"We give no cause for stumbling of any sort, lest our ministry should incur discredit. On the contrary, we seek to commend ourselves as God's servants in every way—by great endurance, by afflictions, distresses, anguish; in floggings, imprisonments, tumults; by toil, sleeplessness, hunger, and thirst; by purity, knowledge, patience, kindness, by the Holy Spirit, by sincere love; by truthful speech, by the power of God; by the weapons of righteousness in right hand and left; through honour and ignominy, through calumny and praise; regarded as imposters, and yet true men; as unknown, yet well known; as dying, and behold we are yet alive; as chastised, but not done to death; as grieved, but always joyful; as poor but enriching many; as having nothing, yet possessing everything" (2 Cor. 6:3-10, *Weymouth*).

Paul was a *large-type* Christian.

"We have renounced the hidden things of dishonesty, not walking in craftiness, nor handling the Word of God deceitfully; but by manifestation of the truth commending ourselves . . ."

"To Every Man's Conscience in the Sight of God"—

The gospel is clearly proclaimed. It is effectively commended by the life. Thus an irresistible impression is made upon the conscience of man under the all-seeing inspection of Almighty God.

Paul addresses himself not to the intellect, not merely to the emotions, nor the imagination of man but to that which underlies every spiritual faculty of man—the conscience. Elsewhere, he calls it the "inner man."

Conscience, apart from divine revelation, is not enough. History in every land proves that it is not enough. Unless it is enlightened by the Word and the Spirit of God, it will be a false guide and a deceitful comforter. It is but like a lantern on the vessel's mast, casting a little light around, but swaying and turning with every motion of the waves. It is utterly incapable of illuminating the whole course, and directing the ship along safely to its harbor. At times, it may even seem totally eclipsed by the lashing storm, or by its own soot and smoke. Nay, the wise pilot must look beyond the lantern, to the steady, ever-shining pole.

Conscience may be deceived so that it thinks falsehood is right. Some hate the truth because their evil deeds want darkness, and their conscience becomes "seared." Still others are indifferent like Pilate, saying, "Why bother with the truth?" These have a blighted conscience. Others have carelessly moved about in the varying light of their own opinions and suffer from a sluggish conscience. Some seem to carry their conscience loose in their pockets as small change for merchandising purposes. It is interesting to note that the phrase in our text "every man's conscience," is the Greek idiom, more accurately rendered, "every conscience of men." This takes them all in, and suggests that whether the conscience is defiled, or crude, or blighted, or passive, it is nevertheless, when aroused, the center of spiritual discernment.

The Apostle appeals to the conscience, but he summons it "in the sight of God." God is watching how each man's conscience reacts to the truth of His Word. This alerts the conscience as no kind of human effort could. The man is in the presence of God. He is accountable to God. The conscience is thus aroused to play it straight.

An aroused, honest conscience should respond to the witness of God's Word, just like the petals of the rose open up to the bathing of the sun upon it. The conscience may be bribed or blindfolded or restrained in the dark, but when enlightened by the truth of God's Word it decrees righteous judgment. It respects and receives the Word, since the Word as well as the conscience are alike of divine origin.

Why are not all men saved, then, after they have heard the truth of the gospel clearly proclaimed and effectively exhibited in the life of a consistent, godly person?

The answer is simple: they refuse to heed the instruction of the truth, and the voice of their own conscience. They choose to oppose the truth and to disregard the pleading of their own conscience. Herein comes the meaning of the Apostle's earlier word to these very Corinthians, "I live for God as the fragrance of Christ breathed alike on those who are being saved and on those who are perishing, to the one a deadly fragrance that makes for death, to the other a vital fragrance that makes for life" (2 Cor. 2:15, 16, *Moffat*).

The case of those who reject the truth of the gospel is one of spiritual blindness. Conscience is on the side of the truth; intellect on the side of the senses. Conscience entreats, warns, condemns, in the name and in the presence of God; intellect is sophistical and stubborn in the behalf of the carnal man. And the intellect is thus alienated from its proper subordination to a ruling conscience by an usurper, who is Satan, the "god of this world, who has blinded the minds of them which believe not."

But in the face of all blindness and Satanic opposition, we "preach the Word." We herald the truth, we "manifest" the truth, we commend it with our whole life, we beseech God to use it for the salvation of souls, and for the building up of believers. But it is God who "giveth the increase." It is His responsibility to give life, and to make new creations in Christ Jesus.

In such a ministry, "we faint not." We know that we have received mercy. We know it works. The process of this ministry involves frequent suffering, and much unpleasantness to the flesh. It involves a continual judging of ourselves, continual renouncing of the hidden things of dishonesty, and continual disavowal of any confidence in the flesh.

In 2 Corinthians 4:7-11, we see ourselves in our weakness as "earthen vessels," "troubled on every side," "perplexed," "persecuted," "cast down," "always bearing about in the body the dying of the Lord Jesus," "always delivered unto death for Jesus' sake." But it is not a waste. It is not loss. It is not defeat. God is working in us and through us "both to will and to do of His good pleasure." In these earthen vessels we may witness: "the excellency of the power of God" wherein we are "not distressed," "not in despair," "not forsaken," "not destroyed," but "the life also of Jesus might be made manifest in our body."

The submissive, yielded life of the believer is in a sense a repetition of the life of Christ, a filling up "that which is behind of the afflictions of Christ" in our flesh. Our troubles and our sorrows, our spiritual warfare in "casting down imaginations," and "bringing into captivity every thought to the obedience of Christ," are as the dying of the Lord Jesus.

But we neither relish the suffering nor consider it as an attainment in itself. Our concern is that against the dark background of our pain, the risen, triumphant life of Christ might shine forth. We have no strength. We have no power. In our flesh dwelleth no good thing. Our hearts are deceitful. Our best resolves crumble. We recognize it to be so. We are convinced that "our sufficiency is not of ourselves." So we come to the end of ourselves and with thanksgiving turn to God who "always causeth us to triumph in Christ, and maketh manifest the savour of His knowledge by us" (2 Cor. 2:14).

Against the background of such submission, God is able to produce the fragrance of divine patience and divine sweetness. In the hour of our most bitter disappointment we are given the opportunity to exhibit before men our trust in God. For "though the outward man perish, yet the inward man is renewed day by day." God knows how to give—

"Secret refreshings that repair your strength,
And fainting spirits uphold."

Chapter III

The Subtle Strategy of Satan

"But if our gospel be hid, it is hid to them that are lost: In whom the god of this world hath blinded the minds of them which believe not, lest the light of the glorious gospel of Christ, who is the image of God, should shine unto them" (2 Cor. 4:3, 4).

This tremendous passage is rendered by *Weymouth* more forcefully, "If, indeed, our gospel is veiled, the veil is on the heart of those who are perishing, in whom the god of this world has blinded their unbelieving minds so as to shut out the radiance of the gospel of the glory of Christ, who is the image of God."

"Our Gospel"

God has but one plan to redeem man, and this is the plan that the Apostle here terms, "our gospel." The essence of this gospel is that Christ died on the cross for the sins of the world, that He was raised from the dead for our justification, and thereby God freely justifies from sin all those who receive Christ, and bestows upon them His own perfect righteousness. "The gospel ... is the power of God unto salvation to every one that believeth" (Rom. 1:16). This is *good news*. This is the greatest beneficence Heaven could give to sinful mankind.

Christ, and the precious revelation of His saving grace, is what the Apostle calls the "mystery of the faith" (1 Tim. 3:9). The greatness of this gospel baffles the unbeliever but it brings the light of solid comfort to every earnest believer. This *gospel* marks the difference between being lost and being saved, and leads inevitably to the great gulf that separates the destinies of the two.

The *gospel* threw light on God, light which before had been unknown. Outside of Christ the purposes of God are enshrouded in deep, dim mystery, and the meaning of eternity is steeped in dreadful silence. The mission of Christ made the love of God intelligible to us; revealed His invitations of mercy with a warm, articulate voice, "Come unto Me all ye that labour and are heavy laden, and I will give you rest" (Matt. 11:28).

The gospel of Christ threw light, also, upon man's own nature, who, until then, was largely a dark enigma, a contradiction to himself, with godlike aspirations and with animal cravings, and withal, confusion and disorder in the soul. "Therefore if any man be in Christ, he is a new creature:

old things are passed away; behold, all things are become new" (2 Cor. 5:17). The gospel threw blessed light upon the darkness of the tomb; for "life and immortality" and resurrection were "brought to light through the gospel."

There is no right knowledge of God but in His Son; therefore, the Scripture says, "He that hath the Son hath life." The Christ of the *gospel* is our *light*, as opposed to all kinds of darkness. He is our light, as opposed to the darkness of Gentile superstitions and idolatries; He is our light in contrast to the dark shadows of the Jewish ceremonial law. As old Simeon said, "A light to lighten the Gentiles, and the glory of Thy people Israel" (Lu. 2:34). He is the light as opposed to the ignorance, slavery and misery of man's natural estate.

The spirit of light and knowledge flows from Jesus Christ into the souls of believers, begetting therein new dispositions and actions, and inflaming their hearts with unfeigned love. Then from the light arises *spiritual joy* and *comfort*, as the Psalmist expounds, "Light is sown for the righteous, and gladness for the upright in heart" (97:11).

It is the *Gospel* in all of its life-giving fulness and power which Satan endeavors unceasingly, and by every means at his command, to pervert, to obscure and to silence.

"Hid"

The better rendering is, "If our gospel is *veiled* . . ." The veil is drawn by the pernicious hand of Satan over the heart and understanding of the perishing.

Men have faculties of vision in several realms. There is the *bodily* eye, from which at least the outward aspects of the gospel are not veiled. They can see the volume that contains it and survey its print. They can look upon redeemed individuals. There is the *intellectual* eye, which discovers the sense and meaning. There is the *spiritual* eye, which at the behest of an unshackled conscience, discerns the practical and personal significance of the truth of the gospel. This is the *veiled* eye, so that the real essence of the gospel is no more discerned by the unbeliever than the bright heavens are observed by the man who is born blind. Therefore, the "natural man receiveth not the things of the Spirit of God . . . because they are spiritually discerned" (1 Cor. 2:14).

This is the precise area where Satan concentrates all his wiles in his wicked intent to thwart the delivering power of the gospel. The glory and illuminating radiance can never be dimmed. Satan cannot hurt the gospel itself, nor can he nullify it. He cannot rob it of its illuminating activity. He can only draw the thick veil over their spiritual eyes, so that the illuminating activity of the gospel does not get to dawn in men's hearts.

These men are not blinded upon any other theme such as music, education, morals, and often they display in these realms much refinement and native ability, while at the same time, they remain totally unimpressed by the revelation of God's wonderful plan of salvation. They seem to exhibit no spiritual capacity whatsoever. "They remain in darkness," as *Lenski* graphically describes "while the light plays around them and seeks to make them glorious with its power."

"Them That Are Lost"

More accurately it says, "to them who are perishing." All men in whose hearts the gospel is veiled are perishing. They are living in a state of darkness, "alienated from the life of God through the ignorance that is in them, because of the blindness of their heart" (Eph. 4:18). They are not aware of their precarious position and the fact that their unbelief, daily, brings them more closely to the precipice of their eternal doom. Soul-ruin is a *gradual* process. They are not hurled there at once. Step by step they proceed down the "broad way that leadeth to destruction." With every day in unbelief, their sensibility of conscience is perishing; their power of the will is perishing. Irrespective of how strong in body, how substantial in wealth and fame, they are decidedly perishing. All their substantial successes are but glow-worms that flash briefly in the dark night of their spiritual ignorance. They already "sit in darkness and in the shadow of death" (Lu. 1:79), and soon to be irretrievably swallowed up in the jaws of eternal death. How startlingly solemn this!

The darkness of the "perishing" is such that they see nothing of real value for themselves in the redeeming gospel of the Lord Jesus Christ. They see no beauty, no glory, no delivering power in the Lord Jesus Christ. Just as the sun, which is much greater than the whole earth, seems smaller than the wheel of an automobile because of its great distance from the earth; so the naturally wise man is deceived by his carnal reasoning in his estimate of Jesus Christ, the "Sun of Righteousness," and the cause is the same,—his great distance from Him. "Thy judgments are far above out of his sight" (Psa. 10:5). He considers Christ and all His glory a smaller matter than his own gain, honor, or pleasure; for these are close to him, and he counts them of far more worth. He enjoys them to the full and rejects with scorn the excellency of the Lord Jesus Christ, which far surpasses the worth of the whole earth, and all things earthly.

The Apostle Paul in writing to the Romans says of the "perishing," that they "became vain in their imaginations, and their foolish heart was darkened" (1:21).

Their hearts become "lodges of vain thoughts," as Jeremiah said. The whole course of a man's life out of Christ, is nothing but a continual trading in vanity, running a circle of toil and struggle, and reaping no abiding profit for himself, nor causing any solid good to come to others. This is indeed blind man's folly, a vain manner of life, receiving only that sure recompense that is due the "unfruitful works of darkness."

It is truly a lamentable thing to be deluded a whole life-time with a false dream, and to be a devotee of a false god. It would grieve any laboring man to work hard all day, and have no wages to look forward to at night. It is a much greater loss to wear out a whole life, and in the evening of our days find only vexation and anguish, and then be led to the "chains of darkness" forever.

Oh, the indescribable folly of the unbeliever! Oh, the inexcusable madness of the "perishing," who are such willing dupes of Satan, the sworn archenemy of their souls! "Satan's promises," said *Mr. Spurstowe*, "are like the meat that fowlers set before birds, which is not meant to feed them, but to take them."

When men have a mind to prefer Satan's lies to the truth of God's revelation, it takes much more than the rhetoric of sermons and the persuasiveness of books to effect their deliverance, though these be administered by the ton.

"The God of This World"

Better translated, "the *god of this age*."

Satan is a subtle and mighty spiritual personality, and the greatest hoax of the universe is his grand deception that he does not exist at all except as a weird, imaginary character in comic strips.

In John's Gospel, Satan is called the *"prince of this world"* three times; he is also referred to as *"the prince of the power of the air,* the spirit that now worketh in the children of disobedience" (Eph. 2:2). There are mighty spiritual forces, arrayed under the leadership of Satan, that war against the higher interest of the souls of men. "For we wrestle not against flesh and blood, but against *principalities,* against *powers,* against the *rulers* of the darkness of this world, against spiritual wickedness" (Eph. 6:12).

Satan, the "god of this age," is a fallen angel, a dethroned principality and power (Isa.14:12-17), and is far from being the mere phantom which he professes. He is so great an individuality whom even "Michael the archangel" did not dare to abuse when contending with him (Jude 9). Our Lord, when tempted by Satan, did not sneer at his folly and make light of his presumption, but commanded seriously, "Get thee hence, Satan" (Matt. 4:8-10).

Though Satan is an usurper, a tyrant, and an insatiable devourer of human souls, the outward aspects of his personality are not those of a repulsive, hideous figure, from which ugliness men would flee by instinct. His is a shrewder cunning a more subtle diplomacy; he "walks up and down in the earth" (Job 1:7) disguised "into an angel of light" (2 Cor. 11:14). When you meet him tomorrow,—and meet him you most surely will,—you will note how he takes on the self-possession of the man of the world, the royal dignity and culture of a prince, the charm and adornment of a "star," the manners of a well-composed gentleman, and the religious airs of a saint. A fine cloak indeed for the most pernicious personality of one who was a "liar and a murderer from the beginning" (Jn. 8:44).

"That old serpent, called the Devil, and Satan, which deceiveth the whole world" (Rev. 12:9), concentrates his skillful activity and prodigious energy upon the one diabolical purpose of drawing the "veil" over the understanding of the unbelievers so that they will not perceive the saving grace of the gospel of Christ.

In accomplishing his ends he exerts all his skill and influence, controls innumerable agencies and organizations, works continually and persistently, and works successfully. Unwearied in his assaults and by force or by stratagem, he detains the souls of men under the "power of darkness," and keeps them captive in the enjoyment of sin.

Satan does not work with every one alike. He knows his advantages, and where men are weakest, and he pursues with acute intelligence after each individual. A conqueror, before he besieges a city, surrounds it at a distance to see where the wall is weakest, best to be battered, easiest to be scaled, where the ditch is narrowest and shallowest, what place he may approach with least danger, and assault with greatest advantage: So Satan goes about surveying all the powers of men's souls, where he may most likely lay his attacks,— as whether the understandings are easily corrupted with error, or the fancies with levity, or the wills with disobedience, or the affections with excess.

One *well known snare* of Satan is making sin pleasant and hiding its horrible consequences.

Knowing wherein his advantages lie, Satan follows with rapacious drive after those poor victims "who are taken captive by him at his will" (2 Tim. 2:26). They seem naturally to grasp after his bait and his line, and fall into his "snare." The snares of the great deceiver are many, but I shall mention here but a few: One *well known snare* of Satan is making sin pleasant and hiding its horrible consequences. A *second snare* of Satan is his insinuating doubts, as with Eve of old, regarding the veracity of God's Word.

A *third snare* of Satan is the hiding of God's justice and condemnation of sin, and presenting Him as all-merciful. A *fourth snare* of Satan is eloquently persuading the soul that the matter of salvation can easily be attended to on the bed of sickness or death. And the *fifth snare* of Satan which captures its millions is his skillful working so as to cause folks to rest in mere professions, in outward forms and rites, instead of the true regeneration of the heart.

As an old writer expressed it, "No player hath so many dresses to come in upon the stage, as the devil hath forms of temptations; but he is most dangerous when he appears in the prophet's mantle, and silvers his foul tongue with fair language." This is so because few people somehow ever suspect the devil to turn preacher. But Satan does, indeed, transform himself into an "angel of light" (2 Cor. 11:14) and becomes a great preacher, a popular preacher, an influential preacher.

He preaches philosophy and politics and morality, and degrades the Scriptures, leaving only a code of ethics, but without spirit and without life and without power "to do that which is good." This wicked tyrant, a wolf "in sheep's clothing," (Matt. 7:15) covers his naked villainy by stealing odd ends of Holy Scripture, "and seems a saint when most he plays the devil."

Expediency and the popular religious trends of the day are also the great themes of exposition by the crafty "god of this age." He exalts the thoughts of the worldly-wise above the divine revelation, and makes his stonified hearers think that they are very much up-to-date. To make up the obvious lack in spiritual depth and understanding, Satan mystifies his flocks with elaborate rites and ceremonies. Mere outward observances are substituted for inward godliness and spiritual communion with the Father.

As a "special boon for those of a more morbid temperament," Satan reserves the austerities of inflicting bodily pain or going into seclusion in order to procure divine favor. And still for others, his dishonorable lowness, the wrong irreverent and ignoble Lucifer, the aged, has the different entangling theories of superstition, and the evil customs of tradition.

Oh the sinister subtlety of Satan! However, we need not be "ignorant of his devices" (2 Cor. 2:11).

"In Whom . . . Blinded the Minds"

"In whom" refers to the "perishing." And the "blinding" the Apostle speaks of does not cover all their thoughts so that they act senselessly in all respects. This blindness involves *chiefly unbelief of the gospel.*

We have in 1 Corinthians 2:14 the astounding statement that "the natural man receiveth not the things of the Spirit of God: for they are foolishness unto him." Now, it is not at all surprising that the natural, unregenerate man does not receive the things of God, but it is shockingly revealing to find that he actually does not choose to accept the truth of the gospel because it sounds silly, something insipid, absurd. It seriously clashes with his own taste; and according to his perverted ideas and pride, these precious truths are but "fables" fit only for children.

Why this strange reaction to God's revelation?

There are many things in the different spheres of knowledge that we do not grasp, but we would have reason to consider ourselves somewhat idiotic if we regarded such knowledge as "foolishness." *Mr. J. Robert Oppenheimer*, a foremost thinker in the development of atomic energy, said in speaking of matter, "The world is subtler than man's understanding, and the contradictions the scientist uncovers in studying nature lie not in nature itself but simply in man's own inadequate concepts."

Why do we not bow down to God who created all this intricate nature at least *with equal respect and dedication of inquiry.* We explore endlessly the fields of natural science, but pronounce the divine revelation of the gospel "foolishness" without any serious investigation. Why? What is responsible for this strange quirk of human mentality? Why is there this obvious rebellion and incapacity to respond to the gospel? Why does a person reveal such reluctance even to talk about the Lord Jesus Christ? People in all walks of life will converse profusely upon any theme, but they become extremely nervous or restless or shut up like a clam, when the theme of salvation is brought in. At once they remember an appointment, become very busy, or wish the doorbell or phone would ring.

Why such abnormal behavior on the greatest subject in the whole wide universe—man's relation to God?

I have spent many hours trying to figure this out, and I always come to the one conclusion as given in Scripture: *"In whom the god of this age hath blinded their unbelieving minds . . ."* Satan has poisoned the springs of human thought and contaminated the fountains of feeling in the human heart, and has created a complex, natural aversion to the truth and reality of the gospel.

This tremendous antagonism has its roots spread out into all phases of life and extends into successive generations. It includes a stream of powerful prejudice, a deep-seated ignorance of

God and ourselves, an unnatural enjoyment of sin, a ridiculous pride, and an unbalanced preoccupation with the things of this world. These are some of the rough components of that thick "veil" with which Satan masterfully blinds "the minds of them which believe not."

We shall now endeavor to examine more closely the vital factors of this Satanic blindness.

First, the stream of powerful prejudice: In 1 Peter 1:18, we read, "Knowing that it was not with perishable wealth, silver or gold, that you were ransomed from the futile habits of life inherited from your forefathers . . ." (*Weymouth*). Those "futile habits of life," inherited from our forefathers, include all the blinding superstitions and vain, unscriptural notions in religion, as well as the corrupt and sinful customs of life. It is easy to fall in line with the errors and practices handed down by tradition because we have a superstitious over-esteem of the authority of our forefathers and also because of the universal sympathy and agreement which those evils have with the depraved nature of man.

In the course of men's lives, the stream of sin runs from one age into another, and every age makes it to swell greater by the accession of tributary brooks; and every human being, when he is born, falls like a drop into this main current of corruption, and so is carried down with its "futile habits of life." By reason of the strength of the current, and the sinner's own nature, which willingly dissolves in it, the course of his life runs true to the evil customs received by "tradition from their fathers." As the prophet Ezekiel observed, "their eyes were after their fathers' idols" (20:24)

The innate prejudices of man toward the gospel of Christ generally rises with him at birth, surrounds him in his infant training, and is solidified into a substantial pattern of life by an early educational bias. The legacy of evil with its strong natural antagonism is handed down to the divine revelation in the gospel of Jesus Christ.

Second: This results in a *deep-seated ignorance of God and of ourselves,* another component of the blinding "veil." The course of life in sin has caused men to "become vain in their imaginations, and their foolish heart was darkened. Professing themselves to be wise, they became fools" (Rom. 1:21,22). This darkness is essentially an ignorance of God and of ourselves. And being ignorant of ourselves, not seeing our own vileness, because we are in the dark, we are extremely pleased with ourselves, and love ourselves instead of God. This self-love, feeding upon the gross ignorance of ourselves, is given by the Apostle Paul as the root of a whole chain of evil dispositions: "For men shall be lovers of their own selves, covetous, boasters, proud," etc., and "lovers of pleasures more than lovers of God" (2 Tim. 3:2-4).

Instead of obeying and pleasing God, they become haters of God. In their darkness they walk "according to the prince of the power of the air . . . fulfilling the desires of the flesh and of the mind . . . by nature the children of wrath" (Eph. 2:2, 3). They learn to like what they see of themselves in the dark; they find that their natural, easy dispositions fit into the pattern of life around them and they become seriously impressed with themselves and with their preferences. They become willing slaves of the "god of this age." Spiritual darkness prevails and disorder reigns in the poor, confused soul, without Christ, without God, and without hope in the world.

Third: This subtle self-love leads to a *cankerous enjoyment of sin.* Men "loved darkness rather than light because their deeds were evil" (Jn. 3:19). The unregenerate heart prefers the husks of Satan to the milk and meat of the Word. Men's hearts are by nature none other than cages of those unclean birds like malice, envy, hypocrisy, sensuality, etc. They are the proper marks of the unrenewed mind, the very characteristics which constitute the image of Satan.

Man's miserable love of sin in its various forms is what entangles his heart, and darkens his perception so that he cannot see the "light of the glorious gospel of Christ." In Kentucky, there is a deep cave which stretches for several miles underground, and is inhabited by blind fish. In preferring the darkness of the cave to the light, these poor fish have lost the power of sight. Eyes they have, but they see not. Just so, man's love of the darkness of sin deprives him of all spiritual vision.

Fourth: Another factor Satan uses in blinding the minds of unbelievers is *just plain ridiculous pride,* which cannot stand "backing down" from a position once openly taken up.

Furthermore, there is something humbling in the first aspects of Christian truth. It brings to our attention our personal shortcomings, and our responsibility. It punctures our bloated spirit of self-sufficiency; it brings us down in the sight of God to the same level of fallen, depraved humanity. "For all have sinned, and come short of the glory of God" (Rom. 3:23). This wounds the natural pride of man who secretly likes to think himself as being just a little superior to all the rest, at least in certain areas.

Fifth: Finally, the evil power of Satan is widely manifest in the *unbalanced preoccupation with the things of this world.* Too eager and too close a contact with the engrossing rounds of secular life becomes an entanglement to the heart. The devil uses even such perfectly legitimate pursuits as art, music, business, sports or home to swallow a man up until he has neither leisure nor desire for the "light of the gospel." By putting a special luster on material things, it is then comparatively easy for the great deceiver to blind the eyes of men to the things which are eternal.

In this same way Satan attempted to blind the thoughts of Christ with respect to the dominion of this world when he showed "Him all the kingdoms of the world, and the glory of them" (Matt. 4:8). All these he offered Christ for the one act of obeisance, "if Thou wilt fall down and worship me."

Satan is the "god of this age." He controls this world system, and advertises his wares attractively; he aggressively parades the glory of this world with its honors and pleasures, and for the seeming small act of submission to himself, he offers these to his victims. And in so doing he estranges the minds and hearts of men from the abiding spiritual realities of God, and his deal in the end proves to be fraudulent and damning. Would you think it a pleasant life, though you had fine clothes and good food, never to see the light of day, but to be kept with your goods in the confinement of a dungeon? This is the circumstance of those who live in worldly honor and plenty, but who are without Christ; they are dwelling in continual darkness, with all their enjoyments, under the enslaving sway of the "power of darkness."

Men who find their all in the world,—fevered by its business, excited by its pleasures, stimulated by its honors,—how can they comprehend the "calm radiance of eternity." They turn away from the interpretations of God's love and God's claims upon them with an indifference that is as weary as it is worldly. They simply do not want to "be bothered" about such things and turn away with a habitual indolence; an indolence which has an uncomfortable misgiving that to listen earnestly might involve further inquiry, and such inquiry might compel action, and that in a direction in which their hearts have no desire to go.

Let not these details of Satan's maneuverings lead us to believe that he is not religious or that he disparages all religion in his followers. That would be far from the truth. As a matter of fact, many of his choicest devotees are not only members of churches but they are also leaders. Satan has no objections to a person being baptized, uniting with the church, singing in the choir, teaching a class or even preaching, so long as that person does not definitely and personally do business with the Lord Jesus Christ on the subject of his soul's salvation.

Frequently, Satan encourages people, whose conscience may be undergoing some arousing, to go join some cold church and forget all about that large debt of unpardoned sin which has been exercising them.

Satan's activities in the realm of religion are the most deadly because his presence there is least suspected. It seems like a very hard thing to say, but Satan has in his control today large, flourishing systems of religion of varying brands. It is fashionable in this twentieth century to be a nominal Christian, and this is due largely to Satan's effective workmanship. Many of his worshippers give passive assent to the gospel of Christ, but there are also those within the organized church who openly and vigorously deny the authority of the Scriptures, the virgin birth and deity of Christ, and the reality of heaven and hell. Let us remember that it was the highly religious groups which opposed and crucified our Lord. It was to these blinded religious leaders that the Lord said, "Ye are of your father the devil, and the lusts of your father ye will do" (Jn. 8:44). This was not a mere accusation; it was a statement of fact.

Although Satan's counterfeit Christianity outwardly passes for the real thing, it is a matter of undisputed evidence that his followers do not have the assurance and joy of sins forgiven; they do not have peace and comfort in their hearts with respect to their eternal destiny, and they do not have the witness of the Spirit that they are the sons of God. Their creed involves glaring contradictions. Their faith is without obedience. Their prayers are without self-surrender. Their success lacks confidence and abiding reality.

Basically the system of Satan differs from real Christianity in the fact of Christ's efficacious sacrifice for sin. The devil has no place for the death and resurrection of Christ, for, in reality, this strikes deadly blows at the old serpent's head. Satan discourages all thought of the blood of Christ, (although he encourages superstitious attachment to a cross or crucifix), because herein lies the delivering power of the gospel.

Satan, using Peter as his mouthpiece, asserted himself vigorously on this subject when our Lord was first mentioning to His disciples the facts of His suffering and His resurrection (Matt. 16:21): "Then Peter took Him, and began to rebuke Him, saying, Be it far from Thee, Lord: this shall not be unto Thee." Our Lord saw, of course, that it was not simply the attitude of his devoted Apostle, and identified Satan to his face, "But He turned, and said unto Peter, Get thee behind Me, Satan: thou art an offence unto Me: for thou savourest not the things that be of God, but those that be of men (Matt. 16:22, 23). A doctrine that would omit or by-pass the atoning sacrifice of Christ for our sin, although it commends itself to man's natural thought, it is, according to our Lord, *not of God* but is Satanic in origin.

Satan's vast counterfeiting system in religion reminds me of the insect that has close resemblance to the "bumble bee," but which is in reality a terrible enemy of it. Because of its close outward likeness, it sometimes finds its way in a fraudulent manner into the bee's nest, and there deposits its eggs. But when these eggs are hatched their larvae devour the larvae of the bees. It has come in as a friend and helper, but turns out to be a devouring enemy. So is Satan!

"Them Which Believe Not"

This Satanic blindness inextricably involves *unbelief in the gospel.* Men's mental reactions to the truth of the gospel are blind. The "thoughts, considerations and conclusions" that arise in their minds upon hearing the gospel are stone-like. When confronted with the person of Christ, their thinking and their reasoning becomes numb, and they act as if they do not see those realities at all. A person is indeed a complete captive of Satan's delusion when he sees nothing desirable for himself in God's saving grace, Christ's blood and righteousness, justification by faith, and all the glorious realities of the new life in the salvation of Christ.

They do not enter into the light and liberty of the sons of God because of the gross blindness which they have acquired through their own unbelief. Their deception is the more impervious because they have a keen taste and a growing desire for the "outward form of godliness." They enjoy and propagate the religion they like, which includes the *fictitious*, the *theatrical* and the *sentimental* factors; but the things that belong to their eternal peace and redemption are hid from their eyes. The counterfeit religion of Satan becomes increasingly attractive to them as it agrees with their own lusts and secret heart-idols.

It is well for us to understand clearly that this blinding "veil" upon the heart of the unbeliever is not an arbitrary thing imposed by Satan. It is self-chosen. The incapacity to understand the spiritual realities of the gospel has been created by continuous unbelief and rejection of Christ at Savior. Throughout His earthly ministry, the Lord Jesus Christ intoned with divine pathos those words which place squarely upon the shoulders of the unbeliever the reason for his doom, "And ye will not come to Me, that ye might have life" (Jn. 5:40).

Someone once said to *Sir Isaac Newton*, "*Sir Newton*, I do not understand; you seem to be able to believe the Bible like a little child. I have tried, but I cannot. So many of its statements mean nothing to me. I cannot believe; I cannot understand."

Sir Isaac Newton replied, "Sometimes I come into my study, and in my absent-mindedness, I attempt to light my candle when the extinguisher is over it, and I fumble about trying to light it and cannot do it; but when I remove the extinguisher, then I am able to quickly light the candle. I am afraid the extinguisher in your case is the love of your sins; it is deliberate unbelief that is in you. Turn to God in repentance; be prepared to let the Spirit of God reveal His truth to you, and it will be His joy to show the glory of the grace of God shining in the face of Jesus Christ."

"Blindness of heart," said *St. Augustine*, "is both sin and a punishment of sin and a cause of sin." God makes the meaning of the gospel obscure to those who delightingly entertain sin. The filthy mists of evil within darken the light of the gospel.

Willful ignorance is fatal. God said through *Hosea*, "Because thou hast rejected knowledge, I will also reject thee" (4:6). There can be no acceptable relationship with God where the light of His Word is despised or ignored. Such a course, if persisted in, leads inevitably to eternal destruction.

Thus we may see that the "veil" of human blindness to the gospel of Christ is something that is self-chosen under the powerful and subtle strategy of Satan, "who goeth about as a roaring lion seeking whom he may devour." This blindness is not an abstract, isolated thing, but it is part and parcel of a vast system of evil under the clever machination of Satan.

A boy in a small suburban town of St. Louis may be induced by a veteran criminal to indulge in a piece of petty thievery, not realizing that he is functioning as a part of a large, well-organized syndicate of crime. But whether he recognized his relation to the crime boss or not, he must stand before the judge and pay for his transgression of the law.

This is a description of the condition of the unbeliever who succumbs to Satan's damning strategy. A meeting was taking place in a great castle situated on the top of a hill. There was a steep cliff, at the bottom of which was a rapid river. Late one night there was a woman anxious to get home from the castle in the midst of a thunderstorm. The night was blackness itself; the woman was asked to tarry until the storm was over, but she declined; next, they begged her to take a lantern, that she might be able to keep upon the road from the castle to her home. She said she did not require a lantern, and rushed out into the darkness. Perhaps she was frightened, or confused, it is not known, but in the darkness, she wandered from the path, and fell over the cliff to her death.

"The Light of the Glorious Gospel"

Literally this should read, "the illumination of the gospel of the glory of Christ . . ." The Greek has here a whole series of genitives to make the subject stand out in all its grandness. The glory of Christ in the gospel is that subject. This glory includes His divine and His human excellencies, and makes Him "the radiant point in the whole universe, the object of supreme admiration, adoration and worship." But the part of this glory which makes it vibrant with life for fallen mankind is the "light" of love and grace that radiates from our Lord's atoning death and resurrection. He died that we might live. He was "made ...sin for us, who knew no sin; that we might be made the righteousness of God in Him" (2 Cor. 5:21). This is the glorious light that pierced the darkness of man's long, depressive night.

This is the light which discovers a man to himself, and lets him see his own natural filthiness, makes him loathe himself, and fly from himself to his all-sufficient Savior, Jesus Christ.

This illumination of the gospel Satan strives to withhold from all his followers. The man of the world may know very much upon many subjects, but he lacks this peculiar light, infused supernaturally into the soul, by which Christ is made known to believers. The unbelievers may discourse and sing about God and His Son and redemption, but they are in the dark, and they see Him not, nor do they love Him.

Just as one beam of the sun is of more worth than the light of ten thousand lamps, so a ray of this heavenly illumination upon the soul is of more value than the speculations and high-sounding knowledge of all the wisdom of man. And a poor, unlettered Christian with the finest discernment, may know more of God than the wisest and most learned natural man can attain to; for the one knows God by God's light, while the other tries to know Him by man's light. As the sun cannot be seen but by its own light, so neither can God be savingly known, but by His own revealing.

Oh the wondrous glory with which this "gospel of illumination" inflames the heart of the believer and fills him with loving estimation of the Lord Jesus! Peter exulted in it, "But ye are a chosen generation, a royal priesthood, an holy nation, a peculiar people; that ye should show forth the praises of Him who hath called you out of darkness into His marvellous light" (1 Pet. 2:9).

It is truly *"marvellous light,"* by the way in which it streams into the soul, and also because of the many excellent things that it unfolds for the believer's enjoyment. If a man were born and brought up in a dungeon, where he had never seen light, and then suddenly brought out into the light of day, what wonder would seize upon him to behold the beauty of this visible world, and the light that makes it both visible and beautiful! How much more admiration there is in the heart of that one who is "called out of darkness into His marvellous light!" Little wonder that the newly redeemed often declare that they live in a "new world," where such wonders of the grace and love of God in Jesus Christ fill their souls.

"Christ, Who is the Image of God"

The relative clause, "who is the image of God," identifies Christ. The meaning of this statement is fully developed in Scripture: "He that hath seen Me hath seen the Father," is what Christ said to Philip (Jn. 14:9). In Hebrews we read that Christ "brightly reflects God's glory and is the exact representation of His being" (1:3 *Weymouth*).

"It is more useful to us to behold God as He appears in His only-begotten Son," said *John Calvin*, "than to investigate His secret essence."

In Christ we behold the only real and direct expression of God. The divine excellencies, particularly God's love for us, are embodied in a living human form. It is this wonderful Person who said, "I am the way, the truth, and the life: no man cometh unto the Father, but by Me" (Jn. 14:6). And a man is confronted with this Person, whom he may accept or reject, every time the gospel is proclaimed. John said, "And the Word (Christ) was made flesh, and dwelt among us, (and we beheld His glory, the glory as of the only begotten of the Father,) full of grace and truth" (1:14).

God created man in His own image and likeness, but through deliberate disobedience man lost this image and lost also fellowship with God. Christ who is the essential image of God, and equal with God, took upon Himself also the form of man that He might give Himself a ransom for us all. Now the love and grace of God are the "gospel illumination" that radiate from Him and which restore the image of God in all those that come to God by Him. This is the message for today—God with us; God for us; God in us; that as we have borne the image of the earthly, we might also bear the image of the heavenly.

The people of the world see no beauty, no glory in Him that they should desire Him, but unto us who are saved "He is altogether lovely" and fills all our vision with the resplendence of heaven.

A scholar once entered the Lutheran Church in Copenhagen to view *Thorwaldson's* world-famous statue of Christ. At first, he seemed critical and dissatisfied. Then a child, aware of his disappointment, explained. "You must kneel down and look up into His face." The visitor followed the child's instruction, and kneeling, he saw the marble masterpiece in a new light. He found a countenance of heavenly beauty directed to him.

And every man who will earnestly humble himself and look by faith at the living Savior, will not only behold the glory of God, but will be "transformed into the same image, from glory to glory, even as by the Spirit of the Lord" (2 Cor. 3:18).

"Shine Unto Them"

It means literally, "should dawn upon them." The illumination of the gospel of the glory of Christ "did not get to dawn" in the lives of those "in whom the god of this age hath blinded the minds." There was no dawning, no morning glow, no bright sunrise, but only the veil of black midnight remained in the hearts of "them which believe not." The fullest sunlight of the gospel produces not even the first dawning for those who choose to remain under Satan's control. The unbeliever thus seals his own eternal destiny in the place prepared for the devil and his angels (Matt. 25:41): "He that believeth not is condemned already, because he hath not believed in the name of the only begotten Son of God" (Jn. 3:18).

A certain tyrant sent for one of his subjects, and said to him, "What is your employment?" He said, "I am a blacksmith." "Go home and make me a chain of such a length." He went home; it occupied him several months, and he had no income all the time he was making it. Then he brought the chain to the monarch, who looked at it and said, "Go, make it twice as long." He brought it up again, and the monarch said, "Go, make it longer still." Each time he brought it there was nothing but the command to make it longer still. And when he brought it up at last, the monarch said to his servants, "It is long enough, take it and bind the poor man who made the chain, and cast him into the furnace of fire." These were the wages of making the chain.

This is a sobering meditation for everyone who thinks it a little thing, a matter of his own innocent preference, to listen to the voice of Satan. Your master, the devil, is telling you to make the chain with which he will bind you and carry your soul into eternal damnation. How long have you been welding such a chain?

Become a Believer Now

Blessed be God, He can break that chain and set you free. "If the Son therefore shall make you free, ye shall be free indeed" (Jn. 8:36). Believe that what God says concerning you and concerning His Son Jesus Christ is true. Take by faith, which is *divine reason,* that Christ died for your sins and rose again for your justification. And even as I write this, I know that these things are unintelligible and unrevealed but to those who are the private scholars and hearers of the Holy Spirit.

Reading the Bible without enlightenment of the Holy Spirit is like looking at a beautiful landscape by the pale light of the moon.

The Holy Spirit wants to enable you to believe firmly that there is *divine truth and power* in the message of the gospel, and to give you a persuasion of it stronger than what you believe of the very things you see with your eyes. This is not a matter of turning on our philosophy and over-powering you, or convincing you with our logic. It is the work of the Spirit of God to open your understanding.

Just now, simply and humbly submit to the Holy Spirit, and try it on one passage of divine revelation: "He that believeth on the Son of God hath the witness in himself: he that believeth not God hath made Him a liar; because he believeth not the record that God gave of His Son. And this is the record, that God hath given to us eternal life, and this life is in His Son. He that hath the Son hath life; and he that hath not the Son of God hath not life" (1 Jn. 5:10-12). There is enough light and to spare in that passage of God's Word to bring about your salvation. And there are folks, no doubt, specifically praying that the glorious light of the gospel will "dawn" in your soul, even now, while the Holy Spirit is striving with you. Amen and Amen!

Chapter IV

We Proclaim Christ

"We preach not ourselves, but Christ Jesus the Lord; and ourselves your servants for Jesus' sake" (2 Cor. 4:5).

A young man had been preaching in the presence of a venerable man of God, and after he had finished, he went to the old minister and said, "What do you think of my sermon?"

"A very poor sermon, indeed," he said.

"A poor sermon?" said the puzzled young man. "It took me a long time to prepare." "Aye, no doubt of it," was the reply.

"Why, did you not think my explanation of the text a very good one?" "Oh, yes," said the old preacher, "very good, indeed." "Well, then why do you say it is a poor sermon? Didn't you think the metaphors were appropriate, the gestures effective and the arguments quite conclusive?" "Yes, they were all very good as far as that goes, but still it was a very poor message."

Almost exasperated, he insisted, "Will you tell me why you think it a poor sermon?"

"Because," said the devoted servant of God, *"there was no Christ in it."*

"Well," said the young man, "Christ was not in the text; we are not to be preaching Christ always; we must preach what is in the text."

So the veteran messenger admonished, "Don't you know, young man, that from every town, and every village, and every little hamlet in England, wherever it may be, there is a road to London?" The young man agreed. "Ah," continued the old minister, "and so from every text of Scripture, there is a road to the metropolis of the Scriptures, which is, Christ Jesus our Lord."

"And, my dear brother, when you get to a text, your business is to say, 'Now what is the road to Christ?' and then preach a sermon, running along that road toward Christ. "And," said he, "I have never yet found a text that has not got a road to Christ in it, and if ever I should find such, I will make a road; I will go over hedge and ditch but I would get at my Master, for the message cannot do any good unless there is a savor of Christ in it."

Jesus Christ is preeminently and gloriously the theme of the entire Bible. All the lines of past human history converge in Jesus, and all of the lines of future history diverge from Him. The all-animating message of divine revelation gathers in and about the crucified, risen Savior, and He stands out upon the sacred pages "as a rich jewel may flash out in a curious, antique setting." From the memorable day when God whispered in the ear of Eve, "The seed of the woman shall bruise the serpent's head," right down to the hour when the angel at Bethlehem announced, "For unto you is born this day in the city of David a Savior . . ., " (Lu. 2:11), we find the reality of Christ pulsating through the divine record, and manifesting itself upon the earth in mighty power, inspiring patriarchs to rejoice in His coming, psalmists to sing His praises, and prophets to declare and herald His coming. And Christ Himself said, "I . . . was dead, . . . behold, I am alive for evermore . . ." (Rev. 1:18).

Christ is the "image of the invisible God, by Him were all things created, . . . by Him all things consist" (Col. 1:15-18). For it pleased the Father to provide reconciliation and peace "through the blood of His cross," that "in Him should all fulness dwell," and "that in all things He might have the preeminence."

One of the consecrated Fathers of the early Church, whose vision was obviously filled with the "Lord of glory," exclaimed, "Were the highest heaven my pulpit and the whole host of humanity my audience and eternity my day, Jesus alone would be my theme."

One day, on his way to Damascus, Paul saw a vision and heard a voice. For three days thereafter he saw nothing, heard nothing, tasted nothing save Jesus Christ. During that time there was burned into his whole regenerated being the all-absorbing theme of his life, which never ceased to vibrate with ecstatic power during all the days of his ministry.

Amidst the whirling controversies of Corinth the Apostle places Him who was ever the keynote of his preaching and his power: "We do not proclaim ourselves, but Christ Jesus as Lord, and ourselves as your servants for the sake of Jesus" (2 Cor. 4:5) (*Weymouth*). Paul wholeheartedly manifested and exalted Christ Jesus as the Lord of his life.

"Two things," once *Goethe* exclaimed, "two things awaken sublimity within me—the starry heavens and man's moral nature." "Two things," Paul might have exclaimed, "awaken sublime enthusiasm within me—the Lord of the Heavens and the new nature He gives to a man." Christ was the source of his new life, the foundation of his hope, the ground of his boast, the burden of his service and the ever-challenging theme of his preaching.

"We do not proclaim ourselves, but Christ Jesus as Lord!"

The alternative is rather clear-cut. If we are not proclaiming Christ, we are definitely engaged in promoting ourselves and our own interests. And let us not forget that this "preaching" is not that of preachers only. All who have become recipients of His mercy are enlisted in this ministry. "Therefore seeing we have this ministry, as we have received mercy . . ." (2 Cor. 4:1). Every believer is to go forth proclaiming Christ Jesus as Lord—proclaiming Him with his life, with his witnessing, with his devotion. In pulpit, in pew—and all the week through—we are to lift up Christ. Our spontaneous conversations during the week are to focus attention on the Lord just as much as our formal teaching on Sunday. Our private enthusiasms are to center in Christ just as much as the public ministrations.

"We do not proclaim ourselves!"

We do not propound our own theories and notions. It was the fault of these factious teachers at Corinth that they taught their own speculations, eyed their own advancement, and promoted their own differing opinions. How sad it is to see fine sincere men substituting the unprofitable theorizings and deductions of men for the life-giving message of the Word of the Lord! This was what the Apostle disclaimed and abhorred, and which every servant of Christ must scrupulously and jealously avoid. It must surely be grievous in the sight of God for a person to project his own ideas before the people in place of telling about the all-sufficiency of Christ. Declare fervently the "grand particularities" of the Christian faith, as *Dr. Chalmers* called them, and you will outlive and outwork those who delight in the pastry of "modern thought."

"But if any speak not concerning Jesus Christ" said *St. Ignatius*, "I look upon them as tombstones and sepulchres of the dead, on which are written only the names of men." The penetrating power and attractiveness of Christianity resides in its all conquering champion, Christ Jesus. *St. Bernard* tells that one Sunday he preached himself, and all the scholars came forward to praise him. The next week he preached Christ, and all the sinners came up to thank him. "We would see Jesus," the hungry multitudes are crying out, whether it be consciously or unconsciously. "The potency of Christian preaching," said *Henry Van Dyke*, "comes from, and is measured by, the clearness of the light it throws upon the person of Jesus."

All sound doctrine converges toward and issues from the excellency of the knowledge of Christ. "Preach the Law," the Jews insisted, and Paul preached Christ the end of the Law to every believer. "Preach wisdom," cried the Greeks; and he preached Christ, the Wisdom of God. "Preach practical virtues, culture, and good conduct," demand the modern critics and other schools of thought; instead we must proclaim Christ who alone can make hearts new, and so make lives pure and godly from the roots. If we leave a man's heart untouched all our admonitions at culture and good morality will be laughed to scorn by the innate weakness and depravity of the human heart.

A young preacher went to *David Swing*, the poet-preacher of Chicago, many years ago, and asked him what he should do to get a congregation on Sunday. He said, "I have tried preaching history, biography, literature, poetry, book reviews, politics—but the people just won't come. What shall I do?"

Swing responded, "Suppose now you try the gospel of Jesus Christ!"

We do not parade our productions, our own talents, our genius, our learning. Our messages are not to be turned into mere dissertations of a philosophical nature. Our sermons must needs be more than just brilliant discourses tailored and trimmed to satisfy the educated taste of an unspiritual generation. Any message, any emphasis, any program—whether it be philosophical or plain, modern or ancient, recommended or unapproved—anything which lets down the curtain between God and men, anything which hides the person of Christ is to be seriously feared and deplored. There are many amidst all our expert programs and high sounding words crying out like

Mary of old, "They have taken away my Lord, and I know not where they have laid Him."

The service of Christ must never be abused for the purpose of displaying our wide learning and exhibiting the profundity of our genius. *Sir Astley Cooper*, on visiting Paris years ago, was asked by the chief surgeon of the French empire how many times he had performed a certain wonderful feat of surgery. He replied that he had performed the operation thirteen times. "Ah, but monsieur, I have done him one hundred and sixty times. And how many times did you save his life?" continued the curious Frenchman, after he had noticed the blank amazement of Sir Astley's face. "I" said the Englishman, "saved eleven out of thirteen. How many did you save out of one hundred and sixty?" "Ah, monsieur, I lose dem all, but de operation was *very brilliant*."

Of how many popular ministries might the same verdict be pronounced. Souls are not saved, but the preaching is very brilliant! Thousands are attracted and operated on by the rhetorician's art, but what if he should have to say concerning the souls of his flocking admirers, "I lost them all, but the sermons were very brilliant."

Paul bore his witness in the plainest and in entirely inartificial language, lest he should so overlay the Cross with the flowers of human rhetoric so that the Christ of the Cross Himself could not be seen. "When I came to you," he told the Corinthians, "I came not with excellency of speech or of wisdom, declaring unto you the testimony of God."

A minister of the past century tells of a Bedouin on a desert who had been without food for so long he was starving. One day he spied a distance away, near a fountain, what he took to be a traveller's bag, and he concluded in his mind at once that it must surely contain bread. Slowly he pulled himself over the hot sand to the little pouch. He took it and eagerly poured out its contents—a stream of brilliant gems. As they wooed the sun by their splendor, his famished body fell over, while he murmured, "Oh, it is only diamonds, only diamonds!"

Merciful heaven, that this should be an honest description of so much that is called preaching! "Diamonds, only diamonds"—glittering words, flashing epigrams, brilliant phrases prettily strung together and tantalizingly dangled before the people who crave plain bread. A tragic thing both for the preacher and for the people! One taste of the "Bread of Life" is much better than all the sparkling sentences, the golden paragraphs and the polished wisdom which all the schools of human learning can grind up! God deliver us from being content to parade our own erudition while souls around us are perishing.

"We proclaim not ourselves!"

We do not merely promote our own organization, our own creed, our own dogmas. We are not to be engaged in serving our church or in extending the distinctive features and accomplishments of our organization. Alas, how sad to see good people busy in religious activities, and yet seriously lacking in spiritual power. The outward activity, with its impressive display is so apt to reduce to comparative insignificance the inward aspects of a person's life. The organization itself becomes the main objective of our life and service; it overtops and thwarts the spiritual realities and purposes it was designed originally to propagate. We become anxious about the success of our society or church. We become absorbed with its successes and its machinery. We gradually lose sight of Christ; and, although we still use His name and reverence Him, our heart devotions are largely drawn out into that which we are accomplishing.

There is one word that covers all such religious activities quite thoroughly: it is *sectarianism*! *Webster* defines a sectarian person as one who is "strongly or bigotedly devoted to the tenets and interests of a particular sect or religious denomination." The ugly selfishness that inheres in the very elements of sectarianism is radically opposed to the spirit of the Gospel. It was a strong sectarian zeal in Pharisaism, the chief religion of that day, that blinded Saul to the claims of Jesus Christ, and spurred him on in his persecution of the believers in Christ. Much activity today which bears the name of Christ is seriously pervaded by this unhealthy zeal and frequently finds its chief impetus at the foul spring of sectarianism. It always steals a person's heart away from the Lord. It never fails to distract attention from the Christ under whose banner we are marching forward. It darkens understanding, it narrows sympathies, it blinds vision, it thwarts the purpose of the Spirit of God.

This destructive, bigoted monster is much more prevalent in our day than we may be willing to admit. Let us be assured that it has more than one change of clothes, and frequently tries to conceal its true identity. It may often be seen when the labors of others are being considered. There should be no envy and no effort at minimizing the success which other organizations and groups are having, but rather there should be a spirit of appreciation and rejoicing in their fruit and blessing. Enthusiasm in our own ministry should never keep us from making an accurate and a generous construction of the work of others. Neither is it helpful anywhere for us to find fault with what others are doing, or to deprecate it by drawing attention to some weaknesses and by raising various suspicions. Such unholy trafficking cannot escape the label of sectarianism and the "woes" which Christ unleashed against such zeal. For by minimizing and deposing others we hope thereby to exalt ourselves.

Frequently it is some pet program, some particular emphasis or some cherished doctrine which trips us up and narrows us down into a sectarian rut. Is it not a hidden brand of sectarianism which vigorously objects to any kind of fellowship with those who differ in the details of theological emphases. It is not necessary for us to scrutinize the motives and to pass final judgment on all the brethren with whom we may be in disagreement. God alone is the infallible judge of their motives and their error. I am not responsible for the failure of those to whom I may extend my hand of sincere cooperation in certain fields of mutual endeavor. "To his own Master a servant standeth or falleth." To follow unyieldingly the course of seeing no good and no point of fellowship with those who differ with me on secondary issues surely marks me with a most undesirable sectarian stripe.

If we consider ourselves as having a fuller understanding of the Word of God than others, if we reckon ourselves as living in the citadel of truth, we can well afford to be generous in our spirit towards the unenlightened ones who are seemingly in error, confident of truth's ultimate conquest and victory. We must needs be uncompromising in the stand we take and the course we pursue, but we can do this without being ungracious and bigoted. Error needs to be exposed and vigorously attacked, but is not this end more thoroughly and more healthily and more profitably achieved by a positive preaching of the message committed to us by the Lord rather than by attacking the personalities and impugning the motive of those who seem to be in error. Truth will put error to flight better than any other weapon. As the poet of another century said, "Truth has such a face and such a mien that to be loved needs only to be seen."

Certain brands of today's orthodoxy are disposed always to look on the bad side. The liberal school has also its "precisionists" who see only the worst in the best men. If a vase is cracked, they are inclined to turn it around and look on the side with the crack. If a vase was cracked, Paul turned it around and looked upon the side where it was not cracked. We are in great danger of losing theological perspective. There were truths dear to the heart of Paul which the Judaizing party in Rome denied and opposed and that in a spirit of contention and strife; their motives were questionable, their error was obvious, and the Apostle was grieved by it, but the small amount of truth that he saw there pleased him more. Even though the opposing party did not love Paul and tried to make his imprisonment more unbearable, yet Paul said, "Christ is preached; and I therein do rejoice, yea, and will rejoice" (Phil. 1:18). His joy did not arise from the fact that certain persons preached, but from the higher fact that Christ was preached.

It is better that Christ should be preached by bad men with doubtful motives than not to be preached at all. While proclaiming the whole counsel of God as it is in Jesus will do far more good, and good of higher nature, than any fragmentary views, yet such is the essential vitality of Christian truth, that its very fragments are powerful and potent for good. Strangely enough much objection against so-called error arises from the fact that it is being promoted by folks who are not members of our association or church. So we wrap up our cheap sectarianism in the velvet garb of defenders of the truth and raise high our voices. But if our relation to Christ is as it should be, the gospel will sound well from any lips—ministers, philosophers, unlearned, and even babes—whether they be in our own organization or outside of it. *Cromwell*, in addressing the Scotch commissioners and Presbyterian clergy after Dunbar—where Cromwell won the decisive victory in 1650—, pressed home this point, "You say that you have just cause to regret that men of civil employments should usurp the calling of the ministry to the scandal of the Reformed Kirks. Are you troubled that Christ is preached? Is preaching so exclusively your function? I thought the covenant and those professors of it could have been willing that any should speak good of the name of Christ?"

Another vast sphere of sectarianism is a certain unhealthy species of church loyalty. *Henry Ward Beecher* once said, "The only difference between a pious denominational spirit and sectarianism is the difference between a cub and a full grown wolf." When the individual becomes absorbed in blind obedience to a denominational body, it corrupts the quality of his spiritual life and service, and ensnares him into a kind of self-interest. He becomes more concerned about total compliance with the suggested program of Boards rather than his full submission to Christ and a careful following of the will of God. But the work prospers outwardly. Members are added. Budgets are increased. New buildings are erected. The public is impressed. The person becomes zealous for the sake of his growing enterprize. Every time he gets an opportunity he boasts about the successes of his cause, his school, his group.

Recently I met a prominent layman, and in our first fifteen minutes together he gave a glowing statistical account of his great church and all the departments thereof. A little while later, a friend joined us and he repeated the boast for his benefit. I listened carefully the second time to see if at least once this brother would mention the name of Christ, or in any way connect with Him their prospering endeavor. Not once did he do so. I managed to restrain a fierce desire to quote to him 1 Cor. 1:31—"He that glorieth, let him glory in the Lord," and I walked away asking myself the question, "Lord, am I guilty of such hollow churchianity too?"

In all such activity Christ is generally not totally excluded, but He is very seriously eclipsed. The eye is not single for His glory. The service, though formally in the name of Christ, becomes earthly and temporal.

Let no one be led to believe by these remarks that the church is disparaged, or its noble mission minimized. No, indeed. The church mission is heavenly, but the machinery for it is very much like the machinery for anything else. Its leaders, its departments, its boards, its committees, its business, its advertising,—all these, in the main, are like the machinery for any other concern. "The church," said *Dr. J. B. Mozley*, "is undoubtedly in its design a spiritual society, but it is also a society of this world; and it depends upon the *inward motive* of a man whether it is to him a spiritual society or a worldly one." May the Lord give us grace to be faithful and true to Himself in all of our fellowship and service!

"We proclaim not ourselves!"

We are not pressing and pushing ourselves for personal advantage. Paul was disappointed in his day in the self-seeking spirit on the part of many servants of God. In commending Timothy to the church at Philippi, he said, "For I have no man likeminded . . . For all seek their own, not the things which are Jesus Christ's" (Phil. 2:20, 21). I wonder if the Apostle was speaking of those who seek out a fellowship or the church which will procure for themselves a certain desired standing in the community and establish good business connections? Perhaps he was thinking of the "Diotrephes, who loveth to have the preeminence among them" (3 Jn. 9).

It is inspiring to see a young man resolutely following the call and commission of Christ. His vision is bright. His spirit is admirable. But how sad to see that young man schooling himself in ecclesiastical politics and already pulling strings for the most lucrative pulpit when he has scarcely completed his formal training! Material advantages and denominational preferment seem to color and at times entirely control his decisions. He abandons, to all practical intents and purposes, the will of God and the fear of God, and in his self-seeking becomes a men-pleaser and a follower of cheap expediency. This is like trying to beat the devil by setting yourself into his hands although no one has ever cheated him in this way. Little by little he sacrifices his convictions and his obedience to Christ in favor of unquestioning, blind loyalty to organization. Perhaps unconsciously so, he finds himself afraid to speak out against anything handed down by his superiors lest suddenly he find himself on the block and swinging over him the loyalty axe, wielded so efficiently by self-appointed Protestant "popelets." He learns quickly that it pays just to go along, irrespective of the issues! Would to God I had never come in contact with it! And I pray that I might be entirely free from such little, hypocritical maneuverings myself.

"We proclaim not ourselves, but Christ Jesus as Lord!"

We proclaim Christ, the glorious, living person. Christianity has organization. Christianity has doctrine. Christianity has messengers. But the force and fount of Christianity is ever the Person of Christ. He gives purpose and vitality to the organization. He breathes reality into doctrine. He makes the messengers flaming evangels. Leave Him out and your Christianity is fatally crippled and takes its place as simply another religion.

Christ's ministry on earth was largely a matter

of confronting people with Himself. He offered Himself to the world as the solution of its complex problems and as the source of new life. Observe how positively, yet how modestly, the Lord ever kept Himself at the front. Without the slightest egotism, the great "I" was ever conspicuous: "*I* am come that ye might have life." "*I* am the way, the truth, and the life." "*I* am the light of the world." His universal, heart-warming invitation centered in Himself: "Come unto *Me,* all ye that labour and are heavy laden, and *I* will give you rest" (Matt. 11:28). This was also the heart of the summary of His completed work: "I, if I be lifted up from the earth, will draw all men unto Me."

It is most interesting to note that Christ's first message on earth and His first message after the resurrection were on the theme of Himself. He entered the synagogue at Nazareth at the outset of His ministry, and having read from Isaiah the prophecy concerning the coming of the great Deliverer, declared unto the people: "This day is this Scripture fulfilled in your ears" (Lu. 4:17-21). Following His resurrection, on the way to Emmaus, "Beginning at Moses and all the prophets, He expounded unto them in all the Scriptures the things concerning Himself" (Lu.24:27). The result was that the disciples said, ". . . Did not our heart burn within us, while He talked with us by the way, and while He opened to us the Scriptures?"

Christ has not changed His program. He still retains this central place. He is still pleadingly offering Himself to weary hearts: "Behold, I stand at the door, and knock" (Rev. 3:20).

> *"Till God in human flesh I see,*
> *My thoughts no comfort find;*
> *The sacred, just and awful Three*
> *Are terrors to my mind.*
>
> *"But when Immanuel's face appears,*
> *My hopes, my joys begin;*
> *His grace relieves my slavish fears,*
> *His blood doth cleanse my sin."*
> *Author unknown*

We do not sacrifice, we do not work miracles at the altar, we do not take philosophical excursions into the wide fields of human knowledge, but we "preach Christ." We present His claims in opposition to the demands of an age one half of which "require a sign," and would degrade the servant of Christ into a priest, and the other half of which calls for "wisdom," and would turn the preacher into a professor. *Macaulay* was right, "Logicians may reason about abstractions, but the great mass of mankind never feel the least interest in them. They must have living images." Indeed, they must have the One who is the bodily, living image of the invisible God. A dying minister looked up at his visitors and said, "If God should raise me up from this sick bed, I should not preach the doctrines less, but I should preach the person of Christ more."

C. H. Spurgeon once illustrated this vital truth in this manner: Suppose that a man has heard of a great physician who understands his complaint. He travels many miles, and when he gets there, they tell him that the celebrated doctor is out. "Then, I must wait till he comes in." "You need not wait," they reply, "his assistant is here." The disappointed, suffering man answers, "I do not care to see the assistant; mine is a desperate case, I want to see the great physician himself."

"Well," they say, "there are his books; you can see his books." "Thank you, " he says, "I cannot be content with his books. I want the living man, and nothing less."

"Do you see that cabinet?" "Yes." "It is full of his medicines." The sick man answers, "I dare say they are very good, but they are of no use to me without the doctor. I want their owner to prescribe for me, or I shall die of my disease."

"But see," cries one, "here is a person who has been cured by him, and has been present at many other remarkable operations. Go into the inquiry-room with him, and he will tell you all about the mode of cure." The afflicted man answers again, "I am obliged to you, but all your talk makes me the more anxious to see the doctor.

I came to see *him*, and I am not going to be put off with anything else. I must see him for myself. He has made my disease a specialty; he knows how to handle my case, and I will not stop till I see him?"

Never be put off with books, or conversations, or preaching, or Bible reading, or prayers offered in your behalf. Anything short of Christ Himself will leave you short of salvation. You must reach Christ, and with the outstretched hand of faith you must touch the living Christ for yourself.

We must never be content to teach or preach unless Christ Himself is the theme. We do not set before people something about Christ, nor somebody that has known Christ, nor some doctrine that extols Christ; but we preach Christ Himself, Christ crucified, Christ risen from the grave, Christ at the right hand of God, Christ returning to receive believers unto Himself. "We preach not ourselves, but Christ Jesus the Lord."

We proclaim Christ crucified. This was the watchword in Paul's preaching and witnessing. "For I determined not to know any thing among you," he told the Corinthians, "save Jesus Christ, and Him crucified." To clear this point up at the beginning I quote *Dr. Buswell*, "It would be better to translate the participle literally in the perfect tense as it stands in the Greek, 'Christ, and Him having been crucified.' " Paul did not preach a Christ now hanging on the cross, but a risen, glorified Christ who had been crucified for us. Paul was a scholar and an orator of the first rank. A mind so spacious and energetic could have glorified any sphere of human learning, yet gathering all the privileges of ancestry, all the advantages of higher learning, all the dignities of office, all the endowments of special revelation, he determinedly made it his business to narrow himself down to the one supreme fact: "Jesus Christ and Him having been crucified." The Apostle purposefully stripped himself of all outward impressiveness which would in any way flatter him and prevent the creative power of Christ's redemption from doing its work in the hearts of his hearers.

The ministry of which Christ is manifestly the center may sweep a wide circumference, and include many subjects. The requirement excludes no province of thought or experience, but demands that all these roads lead up to Christ, whose person and presence shall ever be held preeminent. To proclaim Christ in all fullness is to set forth His person, the story of His sinless life, the fact of His substitutionary death and resurrection, the object of His limitless love,—truths which turn biography into a gospel. Paul proclaimed, ". . . How that Christ died." That is biography and to stop there is not to preach a Savior; but add the rest, "for our sins according to the Scriptures; and that He was buried, and that He rose again the third day, . . ." (1 Cor. 15:3, 4) and you proclaim the good news of salvation! The biography becomes the "gospel which is the power of God unto salvation to everyone that believeth."

Christ, the Savior, must be the undeviating theme of our life, our witness and our preaching. We do not proclaim Jesus Christ the socialist, Jesus Christ the new thought champion, Jesus Christ the wonder of the ages, Jesus Christ either a prospective or retrospective *Aristotle*, but always and everywhere, in season and out of season, Christ the Savior, Christ crucified, Christ shedding His blood that men might not die.

One day early in the eighteenth century, a German artist, *Stenberg,* walking through the marketplace of his home town, was attracted by the face of a dancing gypsy girl. He invited her to come to his studio and be the model for his picture, "Dancing Gypsy Girl." The little girl was much taken with what she saw in the artist's studio, and watched him with great interest as he worked on a painting of the Crucifixion.

One day she said to Stenberg, "He must have been a very bad man to have been nailed to the cross like that."

"No," the artist said, "he was a good man, the best man that ever lived. Indeed, he died for all men."

"Did he die for you?" asked the girl.

That question set the artist to thinking, for he had not yet trusted Christ as Savior. One day he chanced to go to a meeting of the Reformers, who opened the Scriptures to him, and brought him to Christ. He went back to finish his painting of the Crucifixion, working this time not only with an artist's skill and technique but with the love that comes from a believing heart.

When the painting was completed, it was hung in the gallery of Dusseldorf. One day a young aristocratic German count, wandering through the studio, paused before Stenberg's "Crucifixion." The painting moved him greatly, as did the words written under it: "This I did for thee; what hast thou done for Me?" The young count was greatly exercised about his own salvation and about what he should do for Christ. The result was the founding of that noble and fruitful missionary brotherhood, the Moravians. The young count was none other than *Nicholas Zinzendorf.*

And it was Zinzendorf who subsequently, in a time of great spiritual rejoicing and confidence, penned those wonderful words of faith:

"Jesus, Thy blood and righteousness
My beauty are, my glorious dress;
'Midst flaming worlds, in these arrayed,
With joy shall I lift up my head.

"Lord, I believe Thy precious blood,
Which at the mercy seat of God,
Forever doth for sinners plead,
For me, e'en for my soul, was shed.

"Lord, I believe we're sinners more
Than sands upon the ocean shore,
Thou hast for all a ransom paid,
For all a full atonement made."

We proclaim Christ Jesus as Lord, the One exclusive Savior! The revisions are correct in translating it, "We proclaim not ourselves, but Christ Jesus *as* Lord," instead of "Christ Jesus *the* Lord," as the King James version has it. "Christ Jesus *as* Lord" suggests the full redemption work of Christ as *the* one exclusive mediator between God and men, who gave Himself a ransom for all. It is He who redeemed, purchased and won our salvation; it is He who bestows this deliverance upon us through the Holy Spirit, and who makes us His own to live under His dominion in glad and willing submission.

The saviorhood of Christ in this particular connection is further emphasized by Peter as recorded in Acts 2:36, "Therefore let all the house of Israel know assuredly, that God hath made that same

Jesus, whom ye have crucified, both Lord and Christ." The historic Man, Jesus, was approved of God, was crucified, not by accident nor by blunder but by the determinate counsel of high heaven; this Man was raised from the dead and placed at the right hand of God in glory; therefore on such a basis this Man has been made Lord,—presiding administrator—in the realm of salvation. The sacrifice of Himself for the sins of mankind has vindicated the holiness of God, satisfied the justice of God, and forever established His saviorhood. "Christ died for our sins according to the Scriptures," and on the basis of this substitutionary death—the just for the unjust—God has made this Lord and Christ to be unto us "wisdom, and righteousness, and sanctification, and redemption" (1 Cor. 1:30).

This Jesus is Lord of our salvation. He is supreme and unlimited in His ability to save: "He is able also to save them to the uttermost that come unto God by Him . . ." (Heb. 7:25). His word is final: ". . . him that cometh to Me I will in no wise cast out" (Jn. 6:37). His provision positively excludes all other ways, or possibilities, regardless of how good they may sound: "No man cometh unto the Father, but by Me." ". . . There is none other name under heaven given among men, whereby we must be saved" (Acts 4:12).

And the man who is truly convicted of sin realizes with every power of his awakened conscience that God dare not forgive him, that God cannot possibly forgive him except in and through the mediatorial work of Jesus Christ. If God should forgive in any other way it would mean that man has a stronger sense of justice than God. The great miracle of salvation by grace stems freely and definitely and entirely from the Christ of Calvary. The only ground upon which God can forgive the guilt of our sin is the stupendous sacrifice of our Lord's substitutionary death. To put salvation on any other ground is unconscious blasphemy.

How blessedly profound then, and yet how remarkably simple is the gospel of the Lord Jesus. For who can fathom the depths or who is there that can fail to understand the answer to the deepest cry of the human heart, "Believe on the Lord Jesus Christ, and thou shalt be saved"? (Acts 16:31).

"We proclaim Christ Jesus as Lord." The record in the New Testament reveals something of the faithfulness of the Apostles and the early disciples regarding the theme of their life and service. "They went everywhere preaching the word." Let's follow one of them: "Philip went down to the city of Samaria, and preached Christ unto them" (Acts 8:5). Then the Lord directed this deacon to journey to the desert unto Gaza.

Philip went, and there he was amazed to find the Ethiopian prince riding in a chariot and reading from the book of Isaiah. "Then Philip opened his mouth, and began at the same Scripture, and preached unto him Jesus" (Acts 8:35). Oh that we might all be such witnesses, such ministers, such servants of the Most High God.

These early disciples were not propounding their own theories. They were not parading their own learning. They were not promoting their own organization. They were not pushing themselves for personal advantage. They were proclaiming Christ Jesus as Lord in all of His fullness and power! They were not preaching toothless generalities but they were ever confronting people with their Lord and Savior Jesus Christ.

It is Christ alone who can remove the guilt and penalty of our sin. It is Christ alone who can change our sinful nature and create within us new desires after holiness and godliness. Nothing is more impotent than mere ethical and moral preaching disconnected from the efficacious spring of Calvary. Christian morality not only has Christ for its exemplar, but His love for its motive, and His grace for its power. The great Scottish preacher *Thomas Chalmers*, we are told, after having been regenerated in the midst of his ministry— when he turned away from preaching mere morality and began to preach redemption through

Christ—confessed that all his former sermons about man's moral duty had not exerted a feather's weight of influence upon the conduct of his people. It was only when he brought them to the Christ of the cross in his preaching that he was able to note any change in their lives.

"We preach not ourselves, but Christ Jesus as Lord, and ourselves your servants for Jesus' sake." We are serving His interest alone. For His sake we are glad to serve you. He ministered to others; shall not His servant be willing to do the same? We serve unselfishly, never tiring, never complaining, never diverting from our purpose either because of threats or because of allurements. And we proclaim Christ without any ulterior motives. We do not seek to ingratiate ourselves in people's estimation at His expense. We do not use His name for atmosphere and for boosting interest in our organization. We do not talk about Christ in order to gain favor, honor or personal advantage for ourselves. We preach Christ for Christ's sake!

The devoted young saint of God, *Robert McCheyne*, said, "Some speculate about the gospel, rather than preach the gospel itself. I say a man cannot be a faithful minister, until he preaches Christ for Christ's sake." The pulpit—yea, and our every opportunity to witness for the Lord—is to be a pedestal for the cross of Christ and not a mere pedestal for the preacher's fame. We may roll the thunders of eloquence, we may scatter the blossoms of poetry, we may diffuse the light of good ethics and morality, but if we do not make the living Christ the one, overpowering theme of our message, we have forgotten our real mission, and there shall be no abiding fruit. *Rowland Hill* used to say, "See there be no message without three R's in it: Ruin by the fall, Righteousness by Christ, and Regeneration by the Spirit."

May Christ so dominate and permeate each one of us that the whole life shall continuallly be luminous with Christ and our every power and capacity shall proclaim Him in all the fullness of His saving grace—Christ for awakening, Christ for redeeming, Christ for comforting, Christ for sanctifying, Christ for everybody and for every circumstance. And we shall more and more say as did the venerable *Dr. Archibald Alexander*, of Princeton, in his last days, "All my theology is reduced to this narrow compass—*Jesus Christ came into the world to save sinners.*"

Chapter V

God Shined in Our Hearts

"For God, who commanded the light to shine out of darkness, hath shined in our hearts, to give the light of the knowledge of the glory of God in the face of Jesus Christ" (2 Cor. 4:6).

The most satisfying definition of "light" to me is that which was given by a blind man in answer to the question, "What is brightness?" The incident took place at the School for the Blind in the African Sudan, and the question was raised by a man who was blind from birth. Various answers were given but none seemed to satisfy the round table of sightless saints.

Then came the revealing explanation by a man who had been blind since his early youth: "Brightness is that light which God shines in the heart when we put our trust in Jesus as our Savior."

Their faces shone with obvious understanding and delight, and fittingly enough the blind Braille instructor closed his prayer with this clause: "We do thank Thee, our loving Father, for *illuminating* our darkened hearts."

"For God, who commanded the light to shine out of darkness, hath shined in our hearts, to give the light of the knowledge of the glory of God in the face of Jesus Christ" (2 Cor. 4:6).

Here the Apostle traces out the life-giving light of the gospel to its ultimate source—God! The light of salvation shone by a divine operation far superior to that which had, in the beginning, caused the light to shine out of darkness.

Oceans of billowing darkness and chaos enveloped this lifeless world, we are told, (Gen. 1:2) until God sent His omnipresent Spirit to brood over the troubled deep; then the eternal God spoke the far-reaching word, "Let there be light!" Instantly there sprang from its hidden recesses ethereal light, piercing the canopy of the surging clouds and shooting its penetrative influences through their cold masses: *"And there was light."*

At the bidding of the Almighty the cosmic light dawned, the waters retired within limits prescribed for them, the mountains and valleys soon appeared in all their glorious setting. The great lights of the firmament each took its station on high, and began to run its appointed course in the heavens. And so by the creative word of God this world passed from chaos to the wondrous scene of order and beauty which first filled the eye of Adam.

> "Hail holy light, offspring of heaven first-born;
> Bright effluence of bright essence."
> —Milton

"God saw the light, that it was good." Life giving light,—immense, luminous,—pervading all of space and revealing other things, yet itself remaining essentially invisible. Who can explore the secret marvels of light? The waves of light, from four to six thousand in one inch, in undulations of instantaneous swiftness, millions of millions in one second, baffle and confound the human mind. All the tints and colors of nature are deduced from one ray of pure white sunbeam. The strange fusion of light with heat at one end of the scale, and the passage into magnetic force at the other, further alert our curiosity. "Knowest thou the pathway of light?"

Light is distance, amplitude! There is no distance in darkness. Darkness spells limitation. Light is vastness, infinity. Darkness imposes imprisonment. Light is immaterial, diffusive, pure, illuminating. "Physically, it represents *glory*; intellectually, *truth*; morally, *holiness*" (*M. R. Vincent*). The ministry of light is everlasting; it is the condition of all life. It is creative!

"Light!" What is light? Most amazing of all the answer is this: "God is light" (1 Jn. 1:5). A wonderful gathering up into one utterance as to the essential and absolute nature of God—"light." Not *a light*, or *the*, with reference to any created things, but simply, *God is light*, in His very nature. "All that we are accustomed to term *light* in the domain of the creature, whether with a physical or metaphysical meaning, is only an effluence of that one and only primitive *Light* which appears in the nature of God" (*Ebrard*).

John was honored in giving the world the three great revelations: "God is a Spirit"; "God is love"; "God is light." As we consider these declarations of the absolute nature of God, we notice that actually *light* embraces the other two. Light is immaterial and, therefore, readily corresponds to God as *Spirit*. Another inseparable quality of light is radiation and gentle self-impartation, and this, of course, is the very heart of the revelation that "God is love." "Who coverest Thyself with light as with a garment" (Psa. 104:1). Light was the first manifestation of God in creation. The glory of Him who moveth everything penetrates the universe, and shines to the outermost regions. Radiating from Him, light is diffused throughout the entire universe as the principle of life. Without the quickening benefits of light, all would be desert and deadness upon earth. There would be no plants, no crops, no trees. In short, there would be no life of any kind. Light is the sustainer of all life. Light is the ultimate source of all power!

So also does all moral and spiritual and intellectual light proceed from the "Father of lights." He is light, and "in Him is no darkness at all."

The revelation of divine character is as light to His intelligent creation. It is welcome, cheering, illuminating, reviving, life-giving. Our beings find their full satisfaction and enlightenment in the revelation of His mind, which is as the rising of the sun upon our benighted nature.

While still in the Garden, the mercy of God was manifested to Adam in the promise of Redeemer (the "seed of the woman" Gen. 3:15), and in the divinely provided "coats of skin," which required blood-shedding. Then Adam was removed from Eden, but here, too, the light of mercy fringed the judgment of exclusion. "And He placed at the east of the garden of Eden Cherubims, and a flaming sword which turned every way, to keep the way of the tree of life" (Gen. 3:24). The "flaming sword" with its keen edge of holy righteousness protected the "way of the tree of life." Its real purpose was *not* to keep man out of Paradise, but to forbid sin and "aught that defileth" from entering therein.

"The light shineth in darkness, and the darkness overcame it not" (Jn. 1:5 ASV margin). For many centuries the rays of salvation story in the promise of a Redeemer lighted the horizon of this world's dark night. Prophets proclaimed time and again, He will come for a light of the Gentiles; to open the blind eyes, and to bring them that sit in darkness out of the prison house (Isa. 42:6, 7).

And in the fullness of time the Lord Jesus Christ came. "Lo, the star . . . in the east . . . when they saw the star, they rejoiced with exceeding great joy." Truly the "Bright and Morning Star" now shined in their midst, and soon it blazed forth as the "Sun of righteousness . . . with healing in His wings." "The people that walked in darkness have seen a great light: they that dwell in the land of the shadow of death, upon them hath the light shined" (Isa. 9:2). Light, the offspring of Divine power, was now manifest in human flesh, as *George MacDonald* impressively relates:

> *"He, who from the Father forth was sent,*
> *Came the true Light, light to our hearts to bring;*
> *The Word of God,—the telling of His thought:*
> *The Light of God,—the making visible;*
> *The far-transcending glory brought*
> *In human form with man to dwell."*

"Behold, I stand at the door, and knock," He says; note that, *I*, "I stand at the door, and knock: if any man hear My voice, and open the door, I will come in to him, and will sup with him, and he with Me" (Rev. 3:20). He did not send even Postmaster Michael, nor chief of telegraphers Gabriel, not even messenger Matthew or Mark, but "I," the Lord of Glory. As the old colored preacher said of the raising of the widow's son: "He might have sent Peter and He might have sent John, but He just done come Himself."

This God-shining in the heart brings with it a double revelation. It shows by way of contrast how dark by nature the heart is, and how impossible it is for itself to create such soul-satisfying light. It analyzes every act and deed of life, and probes every thought, every feeling and every motive of the soul's activities. It is also a revelation of the character and the presence of God in the heart. It discovers our sin, it searches out our ungodly motives, it shows us the exceeding sinfulness of sin.

I remember vividly, just as if it happened yesterday, seventy-one years ago, one night, lying on my bunk, I understood God's Word. I believed in the Savior. The light shined and suddenly I made the great discovery that I was a great sinner and that Christ is a great Savior. It was as if Christ caught up with me and in His hallowed presence I became keenly aware of the fact that I was lost in sin, alienated from God, condemned, and utterly undone.

And then as I looked up into His face, the light of the glorious gospel of Christ, who is the image of God, began to dawn in my heart. Then I understood the message of salvation, "how that Christ died for my sins" literally and definitely, how it was that "He hath made Him to be sin for us, who knew no sin; that we might be made the righteousness of God in Him" (2 Cor. 5:21). Then I looked at Him again, and like a flash of light from heaven faith leaped forth from my heart, and there and then I, a sinner, committed myself to Him, the Savior! *"And there was light."*

And oh such words of comforting assurance He whispered into my ear. "Him that cometh to me, I will in no wise cast out." "There is therefore now no condemnation to them which are *in* Christ Jesus" (Rom. 8:1).

"God hath shined in our hearts." God radiates the light into all human hearts, but not all experience its gladdening, life-bestowing benefits. As the sun's rays only awaken the sensation of light when they fall upon a receptive eye, so the revelation of God's saving grace must meet with a responsive heart. There must be an eye open to receive the celestial rays and welcome the sacred sunlight. The blind man looks full-face into the sun at midday, and complains, "Sun, there is no sun, I can't see it." Though the light of the Gospel ever shines from the face of Christ, multitudes right here in our own favored land derive no benefit from it. They are preoccupied with themselves, with their own affairs, with their own philosophies. There are still those who are indifferent to the gracious claims of Christ and who prefer darkness to light because of the type of life which they are eagerly pursuing. "The god of this world hath blinded the minds of them which believe not"

(2 Cor. 4:4). When the heart, in simplicity and without prejudice of any sort, turns God-ward like the sunflower to the sun, then the light of the glorious gospel dawns within and brings to fruition a new life in Christ Jesus.

Where this gospel light has not dawned, the soul either ignores or denies the Lord, or, at most, speculates about Him; and at best, it experiences but some spasmodic gyrations of emotional or mental upheaval. But under the radiance of the glad Gospel light, the fact of human sin and the fact of Divine holiness are calmly faced and reasoned, yea and settled forever; and the new creation exclaims joyously, "Once I was blind, but now I see" ". . . I know whom I have believed, and am persuaded that He is able to keep that which I have committed unto Him against that day" (2 Tim. 1:12).

Frequently folks say to the Christian, "How did it happen?" "How did you figure it all out?" "How did it all become settled?" The answer to all such questions lies in the statement, "God hath shined." Only He who could command "the light to shine out of darkness," could cause such reviving light to shine in the sin-darkened heart of man. Humanity could never produce such a light on its own. The light of the Gospel is the light of God Himself. It is God who commanded concerning every believer, "Let there be light." Yes, blessed be God, "and there was light!" It is a definite, direct act of the sovereign God upon the individual soul.

Peter would readily attest to that. Following his confession of the Lord, as "the Christ, the Son of the living God," his faith was promptly analyzed by Jesus Himself: ". . . Flesh and blood hath not revealed it unto thee, but My Father which is in heaven" (Matt. 16:17). Human beings can make partial suggestions by their testimony and by their teaching, but the all-satisfying light is the gift of God. Hence the cry of the saints of all ages has been that God would say again and again, "Let there be light!" Yes, light "in the face of Jesus Christ." Light to illuminate both mind and heart. Light above all other lights—calm, pure, searching, satisfying!

And the testimony of all the redeemed of all ages sounds forth in glorious harmony: *and there was light.*

We are well-acquainted with the record of how this searchlight of God was turned upon a blinded religious fanatic—Saul of Tarsus. This man, a devout Hebrew, a zealous Pharisee, was fiercely opposed to all believers in Christ. Armed with letters of authority, and still breathing out threatening and murderous desire, he was rushing to Damascus to hale men and women "of this way" into prison.

"... Suddenly there shined round about him a light from heaven" (Acts 9:3). At "midday" this heaven-sent light was "above the brightness of the sun," and is not to be confounded with any natural phenomenon. The pressure of this glory-light was so overwhelming that he fell to the earth. The light, like the word of God, was "quick and powerful, and sharper than any twoedged sword" (Heb. 4:12). Along with the arresting, penetrating light there came a *voice*, saying, "Saul, Saul, why persecutest thou me?"

A *"light from heaven,"* a *"voice."* Saul was now confronted with God's Mediator of the new and living way. When the truth of God comes to a person in the power of the Holy Spirit there is always a voice with it, making the sinner feel that he is dealing with a living person and not simply with abstract ideas. Imagine the startlingly and painful surprise that came to this religious zealot, when the "voice" identified itself to him, "I am Jesus whom thou persecutest."

Oh, the convulsion, the upheaval that must have come into the soul of Saul as he began to realize dimly that the brutal stones hurled upon Stephen, to whose death he was consenting, were causing the Lord grievous pain! "Why persecutest thou Me?" This question reveals the terrible blindness of Saul's heart and mind—*he knew Him not.* He knew the Old Testament Scriptures, but he did not know the One whom those Scriptures proclaimed. He was sincere, zealous, but persisted in spiritual ignorance,—"a zeal without knowledge." He was upright, moral, educated, trustworthy, but he resisted the heaven-sent Savior. "I am Jesus, whom thou persecutest." *"I am Jesus!"*

Oh, the tragedy of being a nominal Christian, and yet not knowing, not trusting personally Christ as Savior. It's a life without joy, without peace, without hope! "Ever learning, and never able to come to the knowledge of the truth" (2 Tim. 3:7). "Having a form of godliness, but denying the power thereof . . ." (2 Tim. 3:5) There He stands, the spurned Savior, on the outside of the blinded heart, pleading in the spirit of an ineffable love! Do you know who it is that seeks to possess your life? "Who art Thou, Lord?" He answers: "I am Jesus!" Your silent Friend, your gentle Friend, your closest Friend, your condescending Friend, your understanding Friend, yea, I am Jesus, your *indispensable* Friend! I alone died in your stead; in My own body I bore your sin's punishment that you might live forever!

Christ stood in the path of Saul, and said, "I am the light of the world . . . I am Jesus whom thou persecutest: it is hard for thee to kick against the goads" (Acts 9:5). The light of heaven has been playing about you, impelling you, stirring your convictions. "It is hard for you to kick against the goads"—against the inward urging of God. What are those goads of God? Conscience, the sacred Scriptures, the faithful human ministry, the Holy Spirit! A man cannot be honest and indefinitely withstand the incessant "spur and drive" of such a heaven-empowered team. The light from the Lord is sure to bring captive at the feet of Jesus every earnest inquirer.

> *"Oh Jesus, 'tis Thy light alone*
> *Can shine upon the heart."*
> —*Cowper*

"For God, who commanded the light to shine out of darkness, hath shined in our hearts, to give the light of the knowledge of the glory of God in the face of Jesus Christ." When that light finally dawned upon the heart and mind of Saul, his prejudices melted away in a moment. Why, Jesus was not dead; He was standing before him, gloriously alive, speaking! Jesus was not an impostor; He is the God-sent Savior of the world. Jesus is indeed the Messiah, the promised Redeemer, the effectual Mediator, the Sin-bearer! There was no need for him to try to search out every particular sin as he stood "trembling and astonished" in the presence of Christ; he felt most keenly his sin of unbelief, his sin of persistently rejecting and scorning and opposing the Savior. Now he stood before Him, and his antagonism melted away, his hostility ended. *"And there was light."*

Under the searchlight of God—the presence of Christ—*his faith was instant*: "Lord," he said feelingly, "Lord, what wilt Thou have me to do?" No sooner had he embraced the Lord by faith as Savior, he was presenting himself for service. "What wilt Thou have me to do?" In writing to the Galatians, Paul refers to his conversion in a very striking way, "It pleased God, who called me by His grace, to reveal His Son in me, that I might *preach Him*" (Gal. 1:15).

Christ was so real, so wonderful, so indispensable to Paul, he simply had to tell others about Him. "For the love of Christ constraineth me," (2 Cor. 5:14) he said. Since he was saved he had to proclaim the Savior: ". . . Woe is me if I preach not the gospel!" (1 Cor. 9:16). And the record following up his conversion says, "Straightway, he preached Christ . . ." (Acts 9:20).

Chapter VI

The Supreme Treasure

*"... to give the light of the knowledge
of the glory of God in the face of Jesus
Christ. But we have this treasure in earthen
vessels, that the excellency of the power may
be of God, and not of us" (2 Cor. 4:6, 7).*

The Apostle has just spoken about "the knowledge of the glory of God in the face of Jesus Christ," and then rather unexpectedly, he speaks of a "treasure."

"We have this treasure!"

What is it that the believers have? What is the "treasure" that believers acquire as their own possession. Are they aware of its value? Are they excited about it? Or do they think that the Apostle is simply talking about "things that are not seen" somewhere in the future.

People generally accumulate treasures according to their value in one way or another. The more unique and the greater its worth, the more is such a thing regarded as a treasure. The Bible speaks about treasures, and we want to review a couple of them.

The first one is where God propounded some

hard questions to petulant Job. He said, "Has thou considered the treasures of the snow?" (Job 23:22). What sort of treasure is there to be found in the "snow"? Snow is simply the vapor of water in crystallized form. When the temperature is sufficiently low to freeze the moisture, snow is formed. When this happens in calm air the icy particles build themselves into beautiful stellar shapes, each star possessing six rays. More fully described, snow crystals are six-pointed stars, or hexagonal plates which exhibit the greatest variety of beautiful forms. We are told that some one thousand snowflakes have been examined, and each one was different. Therefore the conclusion that every snowflake is different is not at all unreasonable.

There is in the treasure of the snow a divine order. The entire structure of crystals is based upon mathematical laws and relations. Furthermore, we learn that precise numerical expression exists in the whole world of matter. Each color in the rainbow is due to a certain number of vibrations in a given time. The movements of plants and climbing vines are expressed in mathematical terms, such as ellipses, ovals, curves etc. And who can tell why the feathers in the wings and tail of a bird are numbered according to a mathematical plan in order for the bird to fly. Along with the ancient patriarch *Job*, we stand amazed at how the marvelous variety and beauty of the snowflakes is made according to mathematical order. Whichever direction the human mind turns, as *Henry C. McCook* teaches us, it is brought face to face with the fact that order, mathematical order, geometric order pervades all the arrangements of the universe. And back of all these complex laws stands the supreme Designer—*Almighty God*. In His inscrutable abilities He put these complex laws into all of creation.

The "treasures of the snow" with one accord testify to the *infinite wisdom* and the *supreme omnipotence of God.* They declare His glory.

Then we read about the "treasures of darkness" in the book of Isaiah: "I will go before thee, and make the crooked places straight: I will break in pieces the gates of brass, and cut in sunder the bars of iron: and I will give thee the treasures of darkness, and hidden riches of secret places, that thou mayest know that I, the Lord, which call thee by thy name, am the God of Israel" (Isa. 45:2, 3).

God did for *Cyrus* in 539 B. C. what He promised him through the prophet Isaiah 170 years earlier. He went before Cyrus, made the crooked places straight, broke in pieces the gates of brass and iron built by the Babylonian rulers, and gave him "the treasures of darkness." The expression *does not* mean that the "treasures" themselves were darkness, but that they were hidden in darkness till Cyrus conquered and laid hold of all the vast possessions of Babylon. What a wonderful example of God's *wisdom* and ability to see the future as if it were today.

The "treasure" which believers have in "earthen vessels" lay in darkness until God shined in their hearts the truth of the gospel and gave them "the light of the knowledge of the glory of God in the face of Jesus Christ."

Keep this before you as we turn back in the history of mankind.

Many centuries before, Moses, after communing in the council chamber with his God, said in a great leap of faith and boldness, *"Show me Thy glory."* He failed to remember that "No man can see God and live" (Ex. 33:20). "As well might we expect to bind the winds with cords, or smite them with the sword, as to behold spirits with eyes which were only made to see solid materialism" (*C. H. Spurgeon*). But God did not disappoint His servant. He said, "I will make all my goodness pass before thee." God was about to show His servant a divine attribute—His "goodness." Moses would not see the "face of God" but he would see what God calls his "back parts." This is comparable to the "regal train" which kings have floating behind them. The sun that burns in the heavens with all its radiance and overpowers one is "but a single thread in the regal skirts of the robe of Deity." Such is the brightness of the "back parts," of God when He would display His "goodness." The human body is not strong enough to behold the brilliance even of an attribute of God. Moses was shielded by God in the "cleft of the rock" while the "regal train"—"the goodness of God "—passed by.

We cannot begin to comprehend all the glory of God but we can worship Him.

As we return to our text, it is well for us to realize, as *John Calvin* observed, "that God is not to be investigated in His unsearchable height, for He inhabits the light unapproachable—Eternal, Immortal, Invisible (1 Tim. 6:16), but to know Him as far as He reveals Himself in Christ."

"Father of light!

"Grant such a revelation of eternal glory
    That earthly bliss before its glow shall fade;
That grief may lose its sting and sin its glamor,
    Because our hearts on Heaven are stayed."

This glorious "treasure" may be viewed as (1) a *revelation*, (2) as a *gospel* (3) as a *life*.

First, let us think of the "revelation" of truth that relates to this treasure. Here is a flash of light that sounds the alarm: "For all have sinned and come short of the glory of God" (Rom. 3:23). A long time ago, a small dog was running along a backwoods Kentucky road, yelping frantically because the little dog's master was trapped in an old cave, slowly smothering to death beneath an earth slide. The dog sounded the alarm and the boy, *Abraham Lincoln*, was saved.

The entire human race is trapped by sin, but people generally seem accustomed to it, and think very little of what is happening. When the Communists came to power in Russia in 1917, they revised their dictionary, and "sin" was defined as an Archaic word denoting "the transgression of a mythical divine law." But sin is no myth. Sin is man's sad story—his greatest plight. Sin is sin, and all sin is lethal sin. Sin is suicide. Sin is death. Sin separates a person from God. Sin destroys life and shuts man out of heaven.

In the *revelation* from God we find that the only hope for man is to turn to the Savior, the Lord Jesus Christ, for *immediate and complete* salvation. "He that believeth on Him is not condemned: but he that believeth not is condemned already, because he hath not believed in the name of the only begotten Son of God" (Jn. 3:18).

The "treasure" may also be regarded as the *gospel*, wherein the "righteousness of God" is proclaimed (Rom. 1:16, 17). Redemption is an act of God where the incalculable price for sin was paid by the Redeemer: "For Thou wast slain, and has redeemed us to God by Thy blood" (Rev. 5:9). "For Christ also hath once suffered for sins, the just for the unjust, that He might bring us to God ..." (1 Pet. 3:18). To the Apostle Paul was given the most illuminating word on this subject: "For He hath made Him to be sin for us, Who knew no sin; that we might be made the righteousness of God in Him" (2 Cor. 5:21).

There is no more complete statement concerning the essential truth of the gospel, but neither is there any human parallel of this enormous truth.

John Chrysostom, the "golden-mouthed," in the fourth century, tried to express his amazement at this astounding truth: "What mind can represent these things? God made the Righteous One a sinner, that He might make the sinner righteous. Rather, this is not what it says, but something much greater. He does not say that He made Him a sinner, but *sin*; not only One who had not sinned, but did not know sin, that we might be made, not righteous, but righteousness, and that the righteousness of God.

Martin Luther (1483-1546), a monk in Erfurt, Germany, came alive when the meaning of the Gospel dawned upon him. As he studied the Bible, this divine truth gripped his soul and he pondered it with amazement. "Lord Jesus, Thou art my righteousness, but I am Thy sin. Thou has taken what belonged to me; Thou has given me what was Thine. Thou becamest what Thou wert not in order that I might become what I was not myself."

A supernatural revolution took place on earth some two thousand years ago where Christ died an unspeakable death, but which resulted in the most revolutionary benefits to man. The Bible teaches emphatically that Christ died *in the stead* of sinners and fully met the demands of God's absolute holiness. Sin was laid on Him. He was made sin. He bore our sins, His soul was made an offering for sin, He tasted death for every man (Isa. 53:6; Heb. 2:9; 1 Pet. 2:24). All this was done by our Lord willingly, voluntarily and it was all constrained by love. He loved us and gave Himself for us (Gal. 2:20).

The "treasure" may also be viewed as a *life*. Here, it is obviously the life of the Lord Jesus. "He was made in the likeness of men" (Phil. 2:7), yet He "did no sin" (1 Pet. 2:22). He Himself declared, "I do always those things that please Him" (Jn. 8:29). Speaking of Christ, the record reads, "For such an high priest became us, who is holy, harmless, undefiled, separate from sinners, and made higher than the heavens" (Heb. 7:26). The life of Jesus is characterized by *absolute holiness*.

We could speak similarly, of His wisdom, of His gentleness, of His humility, of His power and of His every other virtue. He lived the perfect life before men and in the sight of God.

However, we want to dwell more fully on His *grace* and His *love*.

There is to be found no more complete description of the grace of our Lord than that which is recorded in 2 Corinthians 8:9— "For ye know the grace of our Lord Jesus Christ, that, though He was rich, yet for your sakes He became poor, that ye through His poverty might be rich." *Grace!* This unmerited bounty from the heart of our Lord becomes the benediction in many of the New Testament books: *"The grace of our Lord Jesus Christ be with you all*: (Rom. 16:24; 1 Cor. 16:23; Phil. 4:23; 1 Thess. 5:28; 2 Thess. 3:18; 2 Cor. 13, 14; Rev. 22:21).

"Marvelous grace of our loving Lord,
  Grace that exceeds our sin and our guilt!
Yonder on Calvary's mount outpoured
  There where the blood of the Lamb was spilt."
                    —Julia H. Johnston

Behold in yonder space "all the saints" "rooted and grounded in love" are gathered for the purpose of knowing "that which passeth knowledge" and are endeavoring to comprehend "what is the breadth, and length, and depth, and height, and to know the love of Christ that passeth knowledge" and "be filled with all the fulness of God" (Eph. 3:17-19). All the redeemed of all generations, of all ages, of all the continents cannot fully grasp all

the dimensions of the love of Christ which is beyond human ability, *but they can worship Him.*
"He loved me and gave Himself for me," and I
cannot comprehend this but *I can worship Him,*
the Lord of glory.

> "Could we with ink the ocean fill
>   And were the skies of parchment made;
> Were every stalk on earth a quill,
>   And every man a scribe by trade;
> To write the love of God above
>   Would drain the ocean dry;
> Nor could the scroll contain the whole,
>   Tho' stretched from sky to sky."
>
> —F. M. Lehman

"Greater love hath no man than this, that a
man lay down his life for his friends" (Jn. 15:13).

The heavens, which He created in His infinite
wisdom and power, declare the knowledge of the
glory of God . The substitutionary death of Christ
for mankind shows us the knowledge of the glory
of God in His immeasurable love.

The face of Christ has more eloquently proclaimed the light of the gospel and the glory of
God than worlds of written volumes ever could.
God shined in our hearts by simply confronting us
with the most glorious Person of all ages, who says,
in effect, "Look in my face and see."

The "knowledge of the glory of God" in all the
facets of Christ's redeeming love is that "treasure."

And here one could wish for "the tongues of angels" in trying to portray adequately the inherent reality and greatness of this "treasure." Let us attempt to define it as the glorious splendor of the Godhead showing itself to mankind in the exhibition of the infinite love of God, in the exhibition of the inexhaustible grace of God and in the exhibition of the everlasting mercy of God. All this is demonstrated by the work of Christ in His substitutionary death and in His glorious resurrection.

Here we have the knowledge of the glory of God in the face of Jesus Christ, and the Apostle calls it "this treasure." It is priceless; it goes beyond all earthly standards of value.

As we think upon it, we recognize with amazement *that this is the greatest treasure in the universe.*

> This treasure I have in a temple of clay,
> While here on His footstool I roam;
> But He's coming to take me some glorious day,
> Over there to my heavenly home!
>
> —Mrs. Will L. Murphy

"We preach not ourselves but Christ Jesus the Lord, and ourselves your servants for Jesus' sake" (2 Cor. 4:5).

An aged saint on being asked to explain salvation, aptly replied, *"Something for nothing."* Another saint, who had weathered the storm for many a year, and was nearing the harbour of heaven, on hearing this related, exclaimed, "Aye it's even better than that, *it's everything for nothing*." True! But to make that possible the Lord of glory shed His precious blood.

> "O the love that drew salvation's plan!
> O the grace that brought it down to man!
> O the mighty gulf that God did span at Calvary!
>
> —Wm. R. Newell

What are the "Earthen Vessels"?

"Earthen vessels" are all those who are recipients of His mercy (2 Cor. 4:1), and who are, therefore, ministers, witnesses, ambassadors of the Lord Jesus Christ. It takes in all the believers. Paul calls himself and all his fellow-servants in the gospel of Christ just "earthen vessels." These were the common, cheap pots made out of baked clay. They were unattractive and had no intrinsic value. Their value lay in what they contained. In the Oriental countries money and other valuables were kept in these earthen crocks, which could be hid, and, in case of danger, might be buried underground.

This figure emphasizes the fragile character of the messengers of Christianity, who are not angels or celestial beings, but the most ordinary of earthly beings. They are frail, imperfect, lowly, weak, unimposing, dying men! They are subject to exhaustion and decay. Their character and judgment are imperfect, and they dwell amidst disturbing and harassing conditions. This was Paul's humble conception of himself. He did not wish to be thought of as somebody important. He was pleased to be only a common container for a priceless Treasure, in order that the Treasure might the more be noticed.

God delights to put His Treasure into unobstrusive vessels. He loves to manifest His power in conditions which excite surprise on the part of those who see it. He likes to kindle the light of His glory on very ungainly lamps. We notice that the early disciples were not from among the "outstanding" men. They were largely common clay vessels, enlisted from the ranks of ordinary men, such as fishermen, farmers, tradesmen. Only a few were men of some distinction.

It is well to remember that the most vigorous in intellect is weak, the most powerful genius is feeble, and the most learned and enlightened is really ignorant. It is the person who *thinks himself wise*, who "seemeth to be wise in this world" (1 Cor. 3:18), that disqualifies himself before the Lord as one who is "vain" and a deceiver of himself.

It is written, "For ye see your calling, brethren, how that not many wise men after the flesh, not many mighty, not many noble, are called: but God hath chosen the foolish things of the world to confound the wise; and God hath chosen the weak things of the world to confound the things which are mighty; and base things of the world, and things which are despised, hath God chosen, yea, and things which are not, to bring to nought things that are: that no flesh should glory in his presence" (1 Cor. 1:26-29).

Although the greatest library of antiquity was in Alexandria, the most distinguished philosophers were from Athens, and the mightiest power was that of Rome, yet in writing the Bible, God passed all these "mighty" ones by, and chose for that purpose one of the smallest peoples of the world. God passed by *Herodotus* the historian, *Socrates* the thinker, *Hippocrates* the father of medicine, *Plato* the philosopher, *Aristotle* the logician, *Euclid* the mathematician, *Archimedes* the father of mechanics, *Hipparchus* the astronomer, *Cicero* the orator, *Virgil* the poet. And why? Because they were wise in their own estimation and were not listening. They were magnificent vessels, and their efforts would attract attention to themselves.

Hence we see God using a pastoral people to accomplish the greatest literary service of all time. Comparatively speaking, they were untaught in the learning of their day. We think of *Hosea* the herdsman, and *Peter*, the fisherman. Peasants and plebeians were the clay pots chosen of God to set forth the priceless truth of salvation.

We need not be disturbed, as *Dr. Roy. L. Laurin* suggests, if the so-called intelligentsia are not following Christ today. There are many earnest believers who fill high and important posts in the affairs of the world, but it is, nevertheless, still true that the roster of God's servants contains "not many wise men after the flesh, not many mighty, not many noble." A lady of royal rank in England, who was a sincere believer in Christ, said she was thankful for the letter "m." God did not say "Not any noble," but "not many."

There was, of course, Moses who was trained forty years in the Court of Pharaoh, but he had to spend forty years in the desert, and we wonder if it were not for the purpose of unlearning the forty years' schooling of Egypt. Paul, similarly, took his spiritual post-graduate training in the School of the Holy Spirit out in the Arabian desert, where he acquired the heavenly perspective so that he could see himself only as a frail vessel of clayware; he was of value only because of the Treasure which he contained.

God likes to show His loveliest flowers in the plainest and most commonplace pots.

The Treasure in Commonplace Vessels.

Why is resplendent treasure seen in common-place vessels?

"That the excellency of the power may be of God, and not of us."

It is a very improper emphasis when the picture takes second place to the frame, or when the ware used at a dinner becomes a substitute for the meal. It is a disappointment to God to have a golden casket of eloquence, which contains no Treasure, no power of the Holy Spirit. Such eloquence is a mere wind-bag; whereas, stammering lips may be declaring the very fullness of God. There is a very real danger that the golden vessel may draw attention to itself, instead of God, just as some of our Easter cards have the cross all wreathed up in beautiful flowers. You think more of the flowers than you do the cross.

God delights to use the commonplace, burnt clay in order that the truth of the gospel may not be obscured by the personal grandeur of the man who proclaims it. "That no flesh should glory in His presence. That, according as it is written, He that glorieth, let him glory in the Lord" (1 Cor. 1:29, 31).

There are numerous and wonderful blessings that proceed from such an arrangement:

(1) That the vessel may know its essential weakness.

When the Lord Jesus Christ revealed to His Apostles the startling truth, "Without me ye can do nothing," He was actually telling them that superhuman strength was required to render acceptable service in His Father's vineyard. The earthen vessel itself cannot do anything for God, and should not attempt to. "Without Me ye can do nothing," but "I can do all things through Christ which strengtheneth me" (Phil. 4:13). That superhuman strength is realized as the believer allows the Holy Spirit to reproduce the virtue and power of Christ in him, and he is then "strong in the Lord, and in the power of His might" (Eph. 6:10).

Oh, how each servant of God needs to recognize his utter inadequacy in himself to do God's work! It is a mortifying fact that the modern Christian ministry, with all its advantages of special training and public respect, actually shows less of heart-compelling power than was exemplified by the early disciples, who were surrounded by such formidable obstacles. They seemed weak, and were strong; we appear strong, and are weak. We need to receive again the word that God directed unto Zerubbabel, saying, "Not by might, nor by power, but by My spirit, saith the Lord of hosts" (Zech. 4:6).

When the Lord graciously crowns our labour with some fruit and blessing, we must, then, the more assiduously guard against the devastating encroachment of self-confidence, "Not that we are sufficient of ourselves to think any thing as of ourselves; but our sufficiency is of God" (2 Cor. 3:5). Thank God that He keeps the check on us, reminding us vividly of our frailty, of our insufficiency, of our essential weakness; hence He causes us to see that, after all, we are only fragile clay crocks, and often, "half-cracked" at that.

Paul, chosen of God for "abundant revelations" and a mighty ministry, was in grave danger of being "exalted above measure." God graciously gave His faithful servant a "thorn in the flesh, the messenger of Satan to buffet" him. Nor would God remove it in answer to fervent petitions, but assured His servant, "My grace is sufficient for thee: for My strength is made perfect in weakness" (2 Cor 12:9). We are not told *what* that "thorn in the flesh" was; perhaps, so that it might the better fit into God's dealings with each one of us, as respecting that infirmity or burden that he gives *us*.

The response of Paul was, no doubt, just what God desired: "Most gladly therefore will I rather glory in my infirmities,"—not because he suddenly began to enjoy infirmities as such, but in order "that the power of Christ may rest upon me." He took pleasure in the varied afflictions and obstacles "for Christ's sake." A new thought dawned upon the Apostle through it, and now it was not ease, nor freedom from burdens, nor even great success that was his goal, but it was the pure desire to enhance the glory of God. He knew that this was the way to bring glory to His Lord. He learned also that this was the way of spiritual strength: "For when I am weak, then am I strong" (2 Cor. 12;7-10).

> "My faith looks up to claim that touch Divine
> Which takes away this fatal strength of mine;
> And leaves me wholly resting, Lord on Thine.
>
> "Make me such an one as Thou canst bless;
> Meet for Thy use through very helplessness;—
> Thine, only Thine, the glory of success!"

(2) That the vessel may be utilized "unto honour"

Recognizing our essential weakness and that "our sufficiency is of God," we do not thereby become careless with respect to the upkeep of "the vessel." Let us always remember the contents. Let us not forget that the "earthen vessel" bears "the Treasure" of heaven, and we want to be the more meticulous about keeping the vessel always clean, usable, "sanctified, and meet for the Master's use" (2 Tim. 2:21). Our dress always neat, our speech always "seasoned with grace," our thoughts always engaged with the things of Christ—"things that are true, whatsoever things are honest, whatsoever things are just, whatsoever things are pure, whatsoever things are lovely" (Phil. 4:8). The human agency, though utterly insignificant in itself, should, nevertheless, commend the heavenly truth; it should "adorn the doctrine of God our Savior in all things (Titus 2:10).

The clay of God's servant may be *marred* by his carelessness and disobedience, or it may be made useful by his care and his obedience to the will of God. To be chosen by the "Lord of glory" for bearing His *Treasure* on earth is superlative honor for the vessel. The fullest utility of the vessel is realized when there is no restraint exercised on the Divine hand that would fill it continually from a Divine source. The people do not want to see the vessel, but its contents, which the vessel does not originate, but which is given of the Lord. Consciously or unconsciously the people are still saying, as the Greeks of old, ". . . We would see Jesus" (Jn. 12:21). And when the vessel, with its whole "baked clay-self" declares, "He is altogether lovely," it is realizing its God-intended function as a "vessel unto honour."

(3)   That the vessel may be moulded by the hand of God.

"Hath not the potter power over the clay, of the same lump to make one vessel unto honour, and another unto dishonour?" (Rom. 9:21).

Of course He does!

But does not the very thought make our hearts still and submissive in the awesome presence of our sovereign God?

We are only clay vessels. His is the "excellency of the power."

We are the vessels; He is the Potter!

To illustrate the "excellency of the power," the Apostle Paul brings in his own experience: "We are troubled on every side, yet not distressed; we are perplexed, but not in despair; persecuted, but not forsaken; cast down, but not destroyed; always bearing about in the body the dying of the Lord Jesus, that the life also of Jesus might be made manifest in our body" (2 Cor. 4:8-10).

We see here the vessel moulded in the hand of the Potter, human weakness sustained by Divine power, and through it all, the Treasure ("the power of the life of Jesus") is the more clearly exhibited. Our life and ministry here is often beset with great difficulties, with multiplied troubles, with variegated trials, and even with serious mistakes. But this does not mean our defeat! "We are pressed on every side, but we are never frustrated; we are put to it, but not utterly put out: we are persecuted and pursued, but not abandoned; we may be smitten down, but we are never knocked out." Many are the uses of adversity. Our ministry is not wrecked even by the most serious trouble or by scores of troubles. We need never be inconsolable. If we be stripped of ever so much that we value, we know that the hand of God is upon us for good, and that we shall yet praise Him! "And now, Lord, what wait I for? *My hope is in Thee" (Psa. 39:7).*

All these partial contrasts of human weakness and Divine power are condensed in the 10th verse in one great contrast, which presents the two sides in their divinely intended relation to each other: *"always bearing about in the body the dying of the Lord Jesus, that the life also of Jesus might be made manifest in our body."* Paul does not say that he bears about in his body the death of Jesus, but His "dying," which is the process that produces death. The sufferings which came upon him daily in his service for Christ were comparable to those pressures and perils and pains which characterized the life, indeed, the "dying of the Lord Jesus."

Does any servant of God object to "always bearing about in the body the dying of the Lord Jesus"? Do we murmur and complain at the hardships?

Here is the word, "For even hereunto were ye called: because Christ also suffered for us, leaving us an example, that we should follow His steps

. . . But rejoice, inasmuch as ye are partaker of Christ's sufferings; that, when His glory shall be revealed, ye may be glad also with exceeding joy" (1 Peter 2:21, 4:13).

But that was not all. In spite of the pressures and pains of "the dying," the Apostle was victoriously alive. Although perpetually in peril, he was perpetually delivered; perpetually hemmed in, yet perpetually the way was opened before him. What was the explanation? It was the "life of Jesus" manifesting itself continually in the outworkings of his life. It can only mean the life of the *risen, living Christ.* The Apostle experienced the resurrection power of his living Lord in the daily deliverances and renewals of his life and service.

Blessed be God! Why, the very purpose of our suffering and perils is to provide adequate occasion for the manifestation of the resurrection life and power of Christ. Unless we are exposed to serious danger, God cannot deliver us from it; unless we are pressed and perplexed, God cannot bring the needed relief. Our emergencies, our vicissitudes are not an accident; they are by Divine appointment and for Divine opportunity.

The exceeding frailty of the *"earthen vessel"* sets off most advantageously the "exceeding greatness of the power."

My mind keeps turning to the life of *Miss Annie*

Johnson Flint of Clifton Springs, N. Y., as an excellent exhibit of "what God can do with a life so bound and yet so gloriously free." Her deep spiritual teaching, in her mature poetic gift, has brought the succor of God to multiplied thousands around the globe. Before she finished high school, she was seriously crippled with arthritis. *Dr. Rowland V. Bingham*, who frequently visited her, says, "One wonders how she could ever get a pen through those poor twisted fingers," but she was a beautiful writer of more beautiful verse. Although at times when her suffering was most intense, the purposes of God in her life seemed obscure, yet she was convinced that God intended to glorify Himself in her weak, suffering body. Having her pain-smitten body protected with "nine soft pillows," she spoke deeply to the hearts of suffering believers everywhere: "God has not promised skies always blue, flower-strewn pathways all our lives through . . . but God hath promised strength for the day, rest for the labour, light for the way . . ."

For more than forty years, there was scarcely a day when she did not suffer intense pain. For thirty-seven years, she became increasingly helpless. Every joint in her body had become rigid, although she was able to turn her head, and in great pain write her lines.

The Potter makes no mistakes as He moulds

the clay left unresisting in His hand. Her poem, "The Cup," pictures her own life:

> *"The Potter fashioned the Cup*
> *With whirling wheel and hand;*
> *Hour by hour He built it up*
> *To the form that His thought had planned. . . .*
> *From the years that were and the years to be;*
> *And the cup that He fashioned He gave to me."*

Then she states the purpose for fashioning of the Cup, which was that it might hold and pour out the "Treasure" of God's living water:

> *"And the clay is Thine—O Potter—Thine;*
> *But the cup of life Thou hast made is mine*
> *To save or lose, to waste or use,*
> *For a poison drink or a draught divine;*
> *To hold it lightly and fling it away,*
> *Or give it for service every day . . ."*

"All these things are," Annie Johnson Flint would say with Paul, "that the abundant grace might through the thanksgiving of many redound *to the glory of God*" (2 Cor. 4:15).

(4) That the vessel may be easily broken.

Though pressed hard, the vessel is kept safe in the hand of God, bearing the Treasure of the gospel of Christ. Sometimes, God directs the vessel to be broken, even an "alabaster" vessel, that the precious contents may be poured out more effectually.

When we think of the Treasure as a light "the light of the knowledge of the glory of God"—there is a story in the Old Testament which illustrates the meaning of the *broken* vessel.

"And Gideon divided the three hundred men into three companies, and he put a trumpet in every man's hand, with empty pitchers, and lamps within the pitchers (Judges 7:16). So "they stood every man in his place," and at a given signal they blew the trumpets, broke the pitchers, and held the torches in one hand and the trumpets in the other, and shouted, "The sword of the Lord, and of Gideon." At that, we are told, the hosts of Midian "ran, and cried, and fled."

When the earthen vessels ("pitchers") were dashed together and broken into fragments, the light shined in the eyes of the opposing hosts. So the light of the glorious gospel often shines more clearly from a broken body and a contrite heart. Spiritual victories are gained and souls are won, not by the great array of human might, but by the unhindered radiance of the light of Christ, and by the unwavering faith in the commands of Christ. God often has the vessels broken to teach us that, though the *cistern* may break, the *fountain* abides full and free.

(5) That the glory of God may be unhindered.

We live in a day when on every hand there

abounds an unhealthy, Lord-eclipsing veneration of the flesh—the flesh of the "wonderful" preacher, the flesh of the "terrific" singer, the flesh of the "smart," the "personable," the "learned." Yet the Word teaches us that "in the flesh dwelleth no good thing," "that no flesh should glory in His presence," and "he that glorieth, let him glory in the Lord." It is quite sobering to read, "Verily every man at his *best* state is altogether vanity" (Psa. 39:5).

There is something seriously wrong when the vessel robs the Treasure of its glory, when the box attracts more attention than the jewel it bears. How refreshing and soul-nourishing it is to experience the mighty power of God pouring out through an unassuming vessel of plain speech. Such was the simple Bible preaching of *Moody*; such was the soul-stirring song of *Sankey*. There are thousands who can preach and sing better than Moody and Sankey, but they have not that overwhelming power and glory of God. It is not eloquence that is needed. We are not spiritually nourished by the long, dazzling strings of sparkling phrases and cunning alliterations. We want solid food.

There is a form of eloquence that must be scrupulously avoided by everyone who really desires "to feed the flock" and to exalt the Lord. And what is true of our preaching and teaching is also true of our praying. The beautiful prayer may attract attention to itself and turn our admiration upon the suppliant instead of directing our faith and adoration to the Lord. The simple, hesitating, broken prayer of sincere confidence in God reveals a sanctifying, sacred force that evokes from our hearts a spontaneous "Amen."

We like to be able to forget the gifts and talents of the preacher. And while he speaks, we would like to be enabled to think only of our wonderful Lord. I have listened to such. God be praised for such servants of God. Oh, how my soul feasted on the power and presence of the Lord while *Lewis Sperry Chafer*, in his diminutive, frail body, quietly sat at his desk, and with unquestioning childlike faith in the Word of God, he permitted the Holy Spirit to instruct and enlighten our hearts. And when *Harvey Farmer* spoke, a hallowed sacredness and pregnant quietness descended upon the hearers, and they were enabled to worship and to adore the Lord, and to "exalt His name together."

Oh that believers, young and old, would set their hearts *not upon the vain applause* of men, but upon the *abiding approval of God*. "The glory of man as the flower of the grass withereth and falleth away," "but he that doeth the will of God abideth forever." If there is in our ministry the blessing of God, let us not become filled with self-esteem, but quietly "decrease" in the *shadows* and let "the Lord be magnified." God has said that

"My glory will I not give to another." Let it be thus with us! The more He gives of blessing, of riches, of power, of responsibility, let us be the more completely aware of our own worthlessness, and let the blessed Lord have the return of more glory.

There is in our day a very disturbing tendency in the direction of the theatrical, the spectacular manner of dispensing the gospel both in the preaching and in the singing.

More than seventy years ago, *John Henry Jowett* deplored this very tendency, though it was a far cry from the "showy methods" of our day, "I think we are living in a time when the earthen vessel has become a costly exhibit. We like large things, showy things, sensational things, noisy things, while God still delights in the earthen things, and He still chooses 'the things which are not, to bring to nought the things which are.' The spectacular organization is just a splendid emptiness, while some quiet and unobtrusive fellowship is laden with the excellent glory of God."

When we see or hear all this colorful clatter, we are reminded of Elijah's experience "when the Lord passed by": There was the "strong wind," "the great earthquake," the "fire," but the Lord was not in the wind, nor the earthquake, nor the fire, though admittedly these afforded a very impressive display of what seemed to be of God. Yet, the record says, "and after the fire, a *still small voice*." God was in that "still small voice," and "when Elijah heard it," he prepared to receive its message.

Let us seek after the Holy Spirit, the specialist of the "still small voice." Let us "stand still" and behold the glory of the Lord! "O magnify the Lord with me, and let us exalt His name together . . . I will praise Thee, O Lord, with my whole heart; I will show forth all Thy marvellous works. I will be glad and rejoice in Thee: I will sing praise to Thy name, O Thou most High" (Psa. 34:3; 9:1, 2).

On the wall of the guest-room of a Rhenish Mission house in Sumatra a guest saw a prayer, which he translated thus:

> *"Light of eternity, light divine,*
> *Into my darkness shine,*
> *That the small may appear small,*
> *And the great, greatest of all:*
> *O light of eternity, shine."*

I was quietly reflecting on this theme the other day, when this question came, How early in life can a person, who is born of God, begin to comprehend the "glory of God," and have a real interest in seeing it brought about? I remember, some years ago, in camp, when one of the contestants sang a solo, and the rest applauded loudly, how I felt inwardly grieved and proceeded to instruct them on how unbecoming it was to applaud anyone who has been proclaiming the message of salvation in song. I was anxious for them to see the reason for it, and I asked them to tell me why it was so inappropriate to applaud. The answer, given by a boy from Oklahoma of about ten years of age, was to me, both thrilling and revealing. He said in substance, "We do not clap when somebody sings the gospel, because that might take away from the glory of the Lord!"

Oh, that believers had a real passion for the "glory of God."

Fra Bartolomeo, the great Italian painter, threw his paints and canvas away because he thought they were stealing his heart from God. But his fellow-monks said to him, "Why should you not paint again *for the glory of God?*" So he painted those remarkable pictures of gospel scenes and faithful martyrs, which are still seen in Italy, and before which men stand, and even kneel in adoration of the Lord. When his brother-monks bade him to write his name at the foot of each picture, he said, "No; I have not done it for my own glory, but to show forth Christ to men." Instead, he scratched on each work these words, "Pray for the picture, or pray for the painter—for the painter that he may do his work in a better way, for the picture that it may more clearly show the Lord;

and let the name of the artist be forgotten."

(6)   That the glory of God may best be displayed.

"Let your light so shine before men," the Savior says, *"that they may see your good works, and glorify your Father which is in heaven"* (Matt. 5:16). "That they may see your good works": see *yourselves* as little as possible, see your *works* more than yourselves. That they may "glorify"— *Whom?* You? No, but "your Father which is in heaven." A sincere Christian sets upon all his actions the one impress: *To the glory of God!* "All our graces (if we have any) are His free gift," says *Robert Leighton*, "and are given us as the rich garments of this spiritual priesthood, only to attire us suitably for this spiritual service, 'that we should be to the praise of His glory' " (Eph. 1:12).

"Be still my soul," not spasmodically, but constantly, "and see the salvation of the Lord!"

There is a significant word in the Greek that is used only twice in the New Testament; it is the word, "Poiema," from which, by way of transliteration, we get our English word "poem." The word is used in Rom. 1:20 and in Eph. 2:10. In Romans, it is translated, *"the things that are made,"* and refers, of course, to the heavens, which attest to the "eternal power" of the Godhead.

This truth is more emphatically expressed by the Psalmist, who said, "The heavens declare the glory of God; and the firmament showeth His handywork" (19:1). The visible heavens, in all their magnificence and vastness, silently and unceasingly, proclaim His glory who framed them. Then again the Psalmist explains, "When I consider Thy heavens, the work of Thy fingers, the moon and the stars, which Thou hast ordained; what is man, that Thou art mindful of him? and the son of man that Thou visitest him?" (8:3, 4). Here, the Psalmist is previewing something that is a greater glory to God's name than the magnificence of the silent heavens. "O Lord our Lord, how excellent is Thy name in all the earth! Who hast set Thy glory *above the heavens*!" (8:1).

The other use of the word, "poiema," is translated, "workmanship." "We are His *workmanship*, created in Christ Jesus unto good works, which God hath before ordained that we should walk in them" (Eph. 2:10). This is God's other "poem." Insignificant pieces of lost humanity—earthen vessels, if you please—are "saved by the grace of God," who is "rich in mercy," and these seemingly worthless trophies of His grace, "created in Christ Jesus," are called "His poiema," His work of art, His great masterpiece.

That is truly amazing and thrilling to contemplate.

"The heavens declare the glory of God, and the firmament showeth His handywork. Day unto day uttereth speech, and night unto night showeth knowledge!" The heavens witness concerning His power and majesty:

> *"Forever singing as they shine,*
> *The hand that made us is Divine."*

And now God's spiritual lights, His "poiema," created through the redeeming love of His beloved Son, declare His glory: *"He brought me up also out of an horrible pit, out of the miry clay, and set my feet upon a rock, and established my goings. And He hath put a new song in my mouth, even praise unto our God" (Psa. 40:2, 3a)!*

The closing part of that verse (Psalm 40:3) shows how much more far-reaching is the effect of God's redemption masterpiece: *"Many shall see it, and fear, and shall trust in the Lord!"*

Oh, the indescribable wonders of God's wonderful salvation—"the light of the knowledge of the glory of God in the face of Jesus Christ." And that such unspeakable "Treasure" should be placed in these poor "earthen vessels," only fills us with unceasing amazement and wonder. "This also cometh forth from the Lord of hosts, which is wonderful in counsel, and excellent in working" (Isa. 28:29). "For as the heavens are higher than the earth, so are My ways higher than your ways,"

God says, "and My thoughts than your thoughts" (Isa. 55:9). We plant and we water the precious Seed, and often with tears. The Holy Spirit uses that Seed, and souls are born into God's family.

His Word accomplishes His pleasure, and brings "joy" and "peace" and "singing" into many hearts. Best of all, "it shall be to the Lord for a name, for an everlasting sign that shall not be cut off " (Isa. 55:13). That is it! That is the most worthy goal of all our visions and burdens and labours. "And it shall be to the Lord for a name!" That is, really, the *only* worthy goal for the redeemed of God.

Reading the diary of *David Brainerd* recently, I was impressed with his longing for utter dependence upon God, and with his spontaneous concern for the glory of God. He wrote thus on a certain day: "And thus I spent the evening, praying incessantly for divine assistance, and that I might not be self-dependent, but still have my whole dependence upon God. What I passed through was remarkable, and indeed inexpressible . . . All my cares, fears and desires, which might be said to be of a worldly nature, disappeared; and were, in my esteem, of little more importance than a puff of wind. I exceedingly longed that God would get to Himself a Name among the heathen; and I appealed to Him with the greatest freedom, that He knew I 'preferred Him above my chief joy.' "

Blessed be God!

God's servant of old said to God, *"Show me Thy glory!"*

In the fullness of time, God's Son came to this world and "was made flesh . . . (and we beheld His glory, the glory as of the only begotten of the Father,) full of grace and truth" (Jn. 1:14). This *glorious* Son of God "loved us and gave Himself for us" and provided a way whereby He might bring "many sons into glory."

And many, from all kindred and nations, turned to the wonderful Savior, and were given the authority to ". . . become the sons of God, even to them that believe on His name" (Jn. 1:12). Humble, clay vessels, now bearing the priceless Treasure of heaven! "But we all, with open face beholding as in a glass the glory of the Lord, are changed into the same image from glory to glory, even as by the Spirit of the Lord" (2 Cor. 3:18).

More literally this reads, But all of us, believers with no veils on our faces, reflect like mirrors the glory of the Lord, and are ourselves being transformed into His likeness, from one degree of glory to another, since it comes from the Spirit of the Lord!

The veil was removed from the face of the

believer at the moment of his conversion, and he became a gospel mirror which reflects Christ's glory of grace and salvation. But that is not all. Christ's glory enters the believer and transforms him from one degree of glory to another. The word for "transform" is the interesting word, "metamorphosis," which indicates those revolutionary changes which occur in the life-history of the butterfly, which at one stage is an ugly caterpillar, and in the next is "transformed" into the butterfly.

So, as we behold the glory of the Lord, and live in communion and proper adjustment to the Lord, we are progressively changed into the very likeness of Christ, by His Spirit, and pass from one degree of heavenly splendor to another. There is a great fundamental change at conversion, when a level of "glory" is reached, but there is much more glory beyond that. We grow in grace. At first we are "babes in Christ," but we are transformed from one state of development to another until the stature of the "fulness of Christ" (Eph. 4:13).

> *"But with mild radiance every hour*
> *From our dear Savior's face benign*
> *Bent on us with transforming power,*
> *Till we, too, faintly shine."*
>
> *—John Keble*

Although this transformation is now in the realm of the *spiritual*, it is, however, an *earnest* of our bodily transformation. Christ said, "And the glory which Thou gavest Me I have given them . . . Father, I will that they also, whom Thou hast given Me, be with Me where I am; that they may behold My glory, which Thou hast given Me" (Jn. 17:22, 24). Lord, hasten the day when this mortal shall put on immortality.

"Beloved, now are we the sons of God, and it doth not yet appear what we shall be: but we know that, when He shall appear, we shall be like Him; for we shall see Him as He is" (1 Jn. 3:2). These "earthen vessels" shall, then, be transformed bodily into the likeness of Him who now fills them. That will be the culminating "metamorphosis" for the believers.

There it is!

The earthen vessels, redeemed by the grace of God, transformed from "glory to glory" until they are fully adorned in the "brightness of His glory." It is all "of God"! The "surpassing greatness of His power," is shown in these poor sinners whom He redeems by His grace. Therein is God's power displayed in consummate glory.

Hallelujah!